The Law and Medicine: Friend or Nemesis?

ROBERT JAGGS-FOWLER

CStJ MB BS (Lond) LLM FRCGP MFMLM DCH DFSRH DRCOG

General Medical Practitioner and Medical Director

Barton on Humber, North Lincolnshire

Radcliffe Publishing

London • New York

Radcliffe Publishing Ltd
33–41 Dallington Street
London
EC1V 0BB
United Kingdom

www.radcliffehealth.com

Every effort has been made to ensure that the information in this book is accurate. This does not diminish the requirement to exercise clinical judgement, and neither the publisher nor the authors can accept any responsibility for its use in practice.

British Library Cataloguing in Publication Data

A catalogue record for this book is available from the British Library.

ISBN-13: 978 190891 199 5

The paper used for the text pages of this book is FSC® certified. FSC (The Forest Stewardship Council®) is an international network to promote responsible management of the world's forests.

FSC www.fsc.org MIX Paper from responsible sources FSC® C013056

Typeset and designed by Darkriver Design, Auckland, New Zealand
Printed and bound by TJI Digital, Padstow, Cornwall, UK

Contents

Preface

The professional practice of the 21st-century medical practitioner is influenced by an increasingly complex set of laws, regulations, professional codes of conduct and academic guidance. A cursory consideration of the history of the medical profession and its interrelationship with the function of the law might superficially suggest that society has moved from allowing unqualified quacks the freedom to offer unscientific remedies almost without legal boundaries to one of paradoxically restricting, through the application of the law, the autonomy of today's highly qualified medical practitioners, despite their scientifically based practice of medicine.

Through a search of primary and secondary sources within medical, legal, historic and philosophical literature, along with an examination of historic as well as modern case law and statute law, the relationship between law and medicine has been traced from ancient times to the years of Tudor England, on through the last four centuries and into the modern day.

The conclusion is perhaps surprising: being that the autonomy of the medical profession is irrevocably symbiotic in respect to law; and that, far from restricting the modern day practitioner, the law in its various forms has been an invaluable ally throughout the development of the medical profession. Even at this time of historic regulatory reform, the law serves to facilitate considerable autonomy and protection for the modern, responsibly practising medical practitioner.

This book is predominantly based on primary and secondary information identified through a search of the subject literature, the result of which formed the basis of a dissertation submitted in partial fulfilment of the requirements for the degree of Master of Laws (LLM) in Medical Law and Ethics from the De Montfort University, Leicester, in December 2010. The dissertation was awarded a distinction in 2011.

Robert Jaggs-Fowler
July 2013

About the author

Dr Robert M Jaggs-Fowler, Kentish by birth, is a physician, writer and poet who, with his wife, now divides his time between Lincolnshire, North Yorkshire, London and Cyprus. With medical degrees, a Master of Laws degree in Medical Law and Ethics, and currently reading for an MA in Spirituality, Theology and Health, he writes weekly health-related columns for two regional newspapers, a monthly column for a county magazine, has had several short stories, non-fiction and 'filler' articles published and has contributed to an American film script. He won the Lincoln Book Festival Prize for fiction in 2005 and the Fathom Prize for poetry in 2010. He writes book reviews for a major magazine publisher, medical and theology journals, has been a regular contributor for an American travel website, published his first collection of poetry (*A Journey with Time*) in 2008, and is currently working on his first novel. His musical interests include playing the piano, alto and tenor saxophones and classical guitar. Meanwhile, he relies on the practice of medicine to keep the garret warm and to ensure good supplies of printer ink and malt whisky.

Acknowledgements

I am indebted to the many organisations and the numerous, and often anonymous, individuals who willingly offered assistance during the preparation of the original dissertation. The exclusion of any person or establishment from this list is an error of personal omission and oversight, for which I apologise.

In particular, I am grateful to the Librarian and staff of the Royal Society of Medicine, the Librarian and staff of the Brynmor Jones Library of the University of Hull, the Archivist for The Worshipful Society of Apothecaries of London, the Librarian of the Royal College of General Practitioners, the Archivist and staff of Hansard at the Houses of Parliament, and the staff of the British Library, London.

I am additionally obliged to Richard Langworth CBE, author and publisher (http://richardlangworth.com), for his assistance in supplying the source and text of Sir Winston Churchill's speech to the Royal College of Physicians of London.

Furthermore, I wish to acknowledge the guidance of my tutor, Dr Ash Samanta LLB FRCP, Senior Lecturer at De Montfort University, Leicester, whose objective view and suggestions were most valuable.

Ultimately, I am once again beholden to my wife, Linda, for her unwavering support and encouragement, practical assistance and immense forbearance throughout my studies for the LLM, during the preparation of the dissertation and this subsequent book.

Permissions

The quotation in Chapter 4 from *Medical Conflicts in Early Modern London: patronage, physicians, and irregular practitioners 1550–1640* by Margaret Pelling (2003) is reproduced by permission of Oxford University Press.

The quotation in Chapter 5 from *Quacks, Fakers and Charlatans in Medicine* by Roy Porter (1989) is reproduced by kind permission of the author.

The verse from Sir Zachary Cope's poem, 'The Story of The Worshipful Society of Apothecaries of London' is reproduced in Chapter 5 by kind permission of The Master and Wardens of The Worshipful Society of Apothecaries, London.

The quotation in Chapter 6 from *Medical Law* by Ian Kennedy and Andrew Grubb (2000) is reproduced by permission of Oxford University Press.

For my wife

Linda

With my ineffable love and immense gratitude

Chapter 1
Introduction

> 'The word "freedom" means for me not a point of departure but a genuine point of arrival. The point of departure is defined by the word "order". Freedom cannot exist without the concept of order.'[1,2]
>
> **Prince Metternich, Austrian statesman (1773–1859)**

THE QUESTION MAY WELL BE ASKED AS TO WHY AN UNDERSTANDing of the relationship between medicine and the law is important. The naive may suggest that the medical profession is a separate entity from the law; although whether that has ever truly been the case is open to doubt, for even healers of the 16th century and before were exposed to public scrutiny and punishment if their treatments did not result in a successful outcome. (Indeed, the Babylonian king, Hammurabi, 1948–1905 BCE,[3] is recorded as the first to delineate the medical profession's civil and criminal liability.)[4] Historically, the training of medical undergraduates is probably largely to blame

1 Prince Metternich, *Mein Politisches Testament*. In: A. von Klinkowstrom, editor. *Aus Metternich's Nachgelassenen Papieren*, Vol. 7 (1880).
2 Elizabeth Knowles, editor. *The Oxford Dictionary of Quotations*. 5th ed. (Oxford: Oxford University Press, Oxford, 1999) 506.8.
3 BCE – Before the Common Era: a term used by historians to 'neutralise' the religious connotations of the chronological label 'BC'.
4 Roberto Margotta, *History of Medicine* (London: Octopus Publishing, [1996] 2001) 10.

for enhancing the errant perception,[5] as it was only in 1993 that the need to include the subject of medical ethics and law in the core curriculum[6] for medical students was formally recognised.[7] However, just as Donne proclaimed that 'no man is an island',[8] neither is the medical profession. Some authors would say that the very idea of 'complete professional freedom' is a fantasy.[9] Everything within a society is, by the very definition of 'society', subject to the rule of law,[10] and if the medical profession is to play its part within society, so too must it follow the rules of the game. During the latter half of the 20th century the relationship between medicine and law certainly became a matter of public interest to a degree never seen before.[11]

If an objective observer of the medical profession in the 17th century compared notes with a counterpart in the 21st century, the conclusion may well be that the medical profession has a consistent track record of persistent resistance to any form of guidance, management, advice, control and regulation originating from outwith the profession. That is not to say that the profession has abrogated its responsibility to regulate itself. Historically, it has been more of a case of 'the doctor knows best' when it comes to what doctors should (and should not) do and how they should do it. Indeed, authorised by Parliament, the profession in England has been self-regulating since 1858.[12] That said, the imposition of regulations, in the form of Acts of Parliament (primary legislation)[13] or Statutory Instruments

5 Harvey Teff, *Reasonable Care* (Oxford: Clarendon Press, 1994) 5.

6 Len Doyle, Medical ethics and law as a core subject in medical education. *BMJ*, 1998; 316: 1623–4.

7 General Medical Council, *Tomorrow's Doctors* (London: GMC, 1993).

8 John Donne, Meditation XVII, *Nunc Lento Sonitu Dicunt, Morieris*, from Devotions upon Emergent Occasions (1623). In: Izaac Walton, editor. *John Donne, Devotions upon Emergent Occasions and Death's Duel* (New York: Vintage Books, 1999) 102.

9 Ash Samanta and Jo Samanta, Regulation of the medical profession: fantasy, reality and legality, *JRSM*, 2004; 97: 211.

10 Geoffrey Rivlin, *Understanding the Law*, 4th ed. (Oxford: Oxford University Press, 2006) 11.

11 Margaret Brazier and Emma Cave, *Medicine, Patients and the Law*, 4th ed. (London: Penguin, 2007) vii.

12 Ibid.: 7.

13 Lorraine Corfield, Ingrid Granne and William Latimer-Sayer, *ABC of Medical Law* (Oxford:

(secondary legislation),[14] from central government has often been met with suspicion[15] if not opposition,[16] and sometimes hostility[17] (including the unusual sight of street demonstrations by medical professionals).[18] Conversely, decisions made within the common law system (i.e. case law developed by judges in a court of law) have more frequently been beneficial to the medical profession, as they demand a logical and objective teasing out of the facts of cases and deliberation as to how the law applies, or should be considered henceforth to apply, to particular situations (e.g. *Re S*[19] and *Bland*[20]). In other words, the judges have often been the arbitrators between the profession and the law of the land, making sense of convoluted, sometimes ambiguous, and at times badly worded statute law, and thus clarifying for doctors the manner in which they can practise lawfully. In addition, apart from protecting the public against unscrupulous practices, the law has also given credence to medicine as a profession, protecting the rights of only suitably qualified persons to practise[21] and, since Sir William Garrow[22] used the Apothecaries Act of 1815[23] to successfully

Wiley-Blackwell, 2009) 2.

14 Ibid.

15 George Szmukler, A new mental health (and public protection) act, *BMJ*, 2001; 322: 2–3.

16 MJ Crawford, W Hopkins, P Thomas, J Moncreiff, J Bindman and AJ Gray, Most psychiatrists oppose plans for new mental health act, *BMJ*, 2001; 322: 866.

17 Daniel Martin, *Doctors' fury at government plans to release private patient data for research*, Mail Online, 22 December 2008 (www.dailymail.co.uk/health/article-1100385/Doctors-fury-government-plans-release-private-patient-data-research.html, accessed: 11 July 2010).

18 Simon Basketter, *Angry junior doctors take protest to the streets*, Socialist Worker online, 24 March 2007 (www.socialistworker.co.uk/art.php?id=10982, accessed: 11 July 2010).

19 *Re S (Adult: Refusal of Treatment)* [1992] 3 WLR 806, where a Caesarean section was legally sanctioned against religious objection.

20 Another example is *Airedale NHS Trust v Bland* [1993] AC 789, where the court sanctioned the withdrawal of artificial feeding of a patient in a persistent vegetative state.

21 The Medical Act 1983, s. 49

22 Sir William Garrow KC PC (1760–1840), barrister, politician and judge; Solicitor General for England (1812–13), Attorney General for England and Wales (1813–17), Baron of the Exchequer (1817–32).

23 The Apothecaries Act 1815. The long title was: An Act for better regulating the Practice of Apothecaries throughout England and Wales.

conduct the first case[24] against an 'unqualified apothecary' in 1819,[25] the law (through Parliament[26]) has assisted in preventing unqualified persons from legally passing themselves off as qualified medical practitioners[27] (despite the legal imprecision of titles).[28]

However, as the law has developed, so too have the boundaries within which medical professionals must work. In this sense, the law has been restrictive as well as protective. With the building of boundaries comes a reduction of freedom; and a reduction of freedom may often be considered as a reduction of autonomy. Unless, that is, the words of Prince Metternich (in the epigraph) are subscribed to; in which case the ability to be truly autonomous is enhanced by having firm boundaries in place. Pitt[29] reinforced such a view by reversing the perspective, quoting Locke: 'Where law ends, tyranny begins.'[30] That said, it may be argued that doctors are not inherently bad people who, without strict regulation, would act in totally amoral ways. However, by setting the bar high for membership of the profession, and equally high for the standard of practice of medicine, the profession is, in effect, giving credence to itself, saying to society 'be reassured – only the highly moralistic, conscientious and meticulous live here'; a fallacy, of course; but arguably a necessary one if society is to respect and trust the profession as a whole. It is a fallacy that is given some degree of credence by the medical profession being prepared to clothe itself in the protective mantle of the law. It is a symbiotic relationship

24 John Hostettler and Richard Braby, *Sir William Garrow* (Hampshire: Waterside Press, 2010) 130.

25 R Percy, 'Anecdotes of the Bar': Learned Apothecary, *The Percy Anecdotes*, Vol. 1. (London: Frederick Warne & Co., 1868).

26 Hansard (United Kingdom Parliament, London 1996) 19 Jan, cols. 1064–9 (www.publications.parliament.uk/pa/cm199596/cmhansrd/vo950119/debtext/60119-24.htm, accessed: 10 June 2010).

27 The Medical Act 1983, s. 49.

28 It is worth noting that the title 'doctor' is not protected in law; however, the term 'physician' is so protected (Medical Act 1983).

29 William Pitt, Prime Minister, 1801.

30 John Locke, *Two Treatises of Government* (London: Awnsham Churchill, 1689) (www.gutenberg.org/catalog/world/readfile?fk_files=28217&pageno=2).

that seems to work; as Brazier and Cave point out, 'few professions still stand so high in public esteem as medicine'.[31]

Although many would claim that the process of licensing and revalidation is a process being rushed through now as a result of various events of the late 20th century, it is an inescapable fact that today's regulation of medical professionals is a product of past events – especially considering that Henry V was the first to act against 'quacks and mountebanks' in 1421.[32] This book attempts to explore the complex relationship between medicine and the law as it developed during the 19th and 20th centuries. However, to put the issues into perspective, it is also necessary to consider developments in the 1600s and 1700s in respect to 'quack medicine', as well as analysing current concerns: what historians might term the 'long 20th century'[33] and, with no attempt at flippancy, a 'very long 19th century'. The question is whether, with the development of laws to protect society against the dubious practices of the charlatans and quacks of the 17th century, there has been a concomitant removal of the autonomy of qualified doctors to practise medicine in whichever way they choose; or whether such apparent 'fettering of freedom' is really a misconception. Is the law really a shackle around the ankle of the medical profession;[34] i.e. medicine's nemesis[35] as an 'inescapable agent of retribution'?[36] Or, conversely, has the law actually been the medical profession's liberator, allowing doctors unprecedented freedom to practise (i.e. enhancing professional autonomy) within

31 Margaret Brazier and Emma Cave, *Medicine, Patients and the Law*, 4th ed. (London: Penguin, 2007) 3.
32 JT Hughes, The licensing of medical practitioners in Tudor England: legislation enacted by Henry VIII, *Vesalius*, 2006; 12(1): 4–11.
33 Arthur Marwick, Introduction to history. In: *An Introduction to the Humanities, The Sixties: mainstream culture and counter-culture, Block 6* (Milton Keynes: Open University, [1998] 2005) 39.
34 Fetter: '1. A chain or shackle placed around a prisoner's neck; 2. A restraint or check.' In: Catherine Soanes, editor, *The Compact Oxford English Dictionary*, 2nd ed. (Oxford: Oxford University Press, 2002).
35 Nemesis: in Greek mythology, Nemesis was the personification of the gods' retribution for violation of sacred laws.
36 Ibid.

a cocoon of lawfulness and respectability? In other words, by arming itself with the rights and protection laid down in law, has the medical profession been enabled to safely flourish in a manner unknown to those struggling for recognition and respectability some three or four hundred years ago? By tracing the history of the interaction of law and medicine, I will attempt to show that, in reality, the latter is the case: the law is, in relation to the profession of medicine, an invaluable friend, without which the medical profession would be denuded of respectability, status and power.

All of which, it may be argued, are prerequisites if medicine is to influence the well-being of modern society.

Chapter 2

Materiae philosophicae

'Man is born Free, and everywhere he is in chains.'[1]

Jean-Jacques Rousseau (1762)[2]

AN EXPOSITION EXAMINING THE HISTORICAL UNDULATIONS OF medical autonomy must, for the sake of lucidity, begin by offering firm guidance as to the meaning of the terminology utilised. As the regulation of the activities of those who were the forbears of the future general medical practitioners of England commenced with the Apothecaries Act in 1815, it would seem appropriate to begin such direction with the freedom philosophy extant towards the mid and late 18th century, i.e. that of Rousseau and the French Revolutionaries.[3]

The quotation at the start of this chapter is taken from the opening paragraphs of Rousseau's treatise of 1762, known in short as 'The Social Contract'. The same words are reflected in the opening paragraph of the French 'Declaration of the rights of man and the

1 Jean-Jacque Rousseau, *Du Contract Social ou Principes du Droit Politique* (Amsterdam: Chez Marc, 1762). In: GDH Cole, translator, *Social Contract or Principles of Political Right Great Books* (Chicago, IL: Encyclopaedia Britannica, [1952] 1990) 35, 387, 1.

2 Jean-Jacque Rousseau (1712–78), Genevois philosopher, writer and composer.

3 The French Revolution, 1789–99.

citizen':[4] 'Men are born, and always continue, free and equal in respect of their rights.'

The term 'rights' is itself of great interest and importance. 'Rights' reflect the permitted activities by, and treatment of, people living within a society.[5] The concept of rights has permeated English, European and American law for the past two centuries, with no greater examples than the Convention of Human Rights,[6] The Human Rights Act[7] and the American Constitution.[8] The rights enshrined within these laws have filtered down to significantly inform the current laws and regulations appertaining to the practice of medicine,[9] especially in relation to subjects such as consent[10] (with particular consideration to older children),[11] standards of care[12] (overlapping criminal law),[13] confidentiality (clearly documented by the National Health Service (NHS),[14] the General Medical Council (GMC),[15] and enshrined in law[16]), medical records (with specific legislation,[17] and a more inclusive approach[18]), mental capacity,[19] mental health (with

4 *Déclaration des droits de l'Homme et du Citoyen* (The National Assembly of France, 26 August 1789), Article 1. (www.hrcr.org/docs/frenchdec.html).

5 Arthur Marwick, Rousseau's Argument. In: *An Introduction to the Humanities, History, Classicism and Revolution, Block 3* (Milton Keynes: Open University, [1998] 2005) 93–9.

6 The European Convention on Human Rights 1950, (long title: Convention for the Protection of Rights and Fundamental Freedoms), established the European Court of Human Rights.

7 Human Rights Act 1998.

8 The Constitution of the United States of America 1787, the first 10 amendments of which are known as the Bill of Rights.

9 *Introduction to Health Care Law and Ethics*, LLM Module Handbook (Leicester: De Montfort University, 2009) 21.

10 *Good Medical Practice* (London: GMC, 2006).

11 Family Law Reform Act 1969 gives a child of 16 years or more the right to consent to surgical or dental treatment.

12 Ibid.

13 Corporate Manslaughter and Homicide Act 2007.

14 *Confidentiality: NHS Code of Practice 2003* (London: Department of Health) (www.connectingforhealth.nhs.uk/systemsandservices/infogov/codes/confcode.pdf).

15 *Confidentiality* (London: GMC, 2009).

16 NHS Act 2006, s. 251.

17 Access to Health Records Act 1990.

18 Data Protection Act 1998.

19 Mental Capacity Act 2005.

Acts in 1983[20] and 2007[21]) and organ retention;[22] although they are equally overridden by specific laws relating to the greater interest of the public and society (e.g. on the subject of abortion,[23] control of infectious disease,[24] criminal activity[25] and terrorism[26]).

Rousseau's reference to 'living in chains' is in essence an allusion to the reality of living within a society. As Cicero is reported to have said, '*Legum servi sumus et liberi esse possimus*' ('we are slaves of the law so that we may be free'),[27] a concept which still echoes in present-day legal philosophy.[28] The freedom gained by living within society (e.g. through the benefits of a ready food supply, education, the provision of health and social services, and protection by police and armed forces) is at the price of the freedom with which Rousseau maintains is our birthright. Doctors live within societies. Societies are 'sets of individuals in relations governed by practical interdependence, convention, and perhaps law'.[29] Whilst having certain personal freedoms within the laws of their society, they are also bound by the general will[30] of that society;[31] it is therefore logical to conclude that doctors can never be autonomous (within their professional capacity) in the purest sense of the word.

Indeed, if consideration is given to the basic concept of autonomy, a problem arises from the very origin of the word. It is derived from the ancient Greek word '*autonomos*', which in turn is composed of

20 Mental Health Act 1983.
21 Mental Health Act 2007.
22 Organ Retention and the Human Tissue Act 2004.
23 Abortion Act 1967
24 Public Health (Control of Disease) Act 1984.
25 Police and Criminal Evidence Act 1984.
26 Terrorism Act 2000.
27 David Johnston, *Roman Law in Context* (Cambridge: Cambridge University Press, 1999).
28 Raymond Wacks, *Law: a very short introduction* (Oxford: Oxford University Press, 2008) 21.
29 Ted Honderich, editor, *The Oxford Companion to Philosophy* (Oxford: Oxford University Press, 1995) 835–6.
30 The 'general will' is a concept formulated by Rousseau, and relates to the desires (will) of a group as a whole, rather than the collective wills of the members of society as individuals.
31 *See* note 29: 306.

the two words '*auto*' (self) and '*nomos*' (law).[32] Together, the meaning is 'one who gives oneself their own law'.[33] It is a word that did not appear in the English language until 1881,[34] when introduced as a metaphysical concept[35] by Kant.[36] If the etymology is to be followed to the letter, the medical profession has never been truly autonomous from the very day Henry V gave recognition to it, and if general practitioners started as the regulated apothecaries of 1815, any consideration of that branch of the profession being autonomous was removed before the word had even been coined.

In relation to the earlier practice of medicine, it may therefore be more desirable to consider the philosophical theory of 'free will', a concept that first came to light (within the English language) as early as 1300.[37] However, the philosophical idea of causal determinism then confounds the issue, arguing that whatever one decides in the future is already influenced by past and present events.[38] Today's doctors may perceive that the profession's autonomy, freedom or free will (however one wishes to phrase it) is being withdrawn by society's reaction to events such as Shipman,[39] and the Alder Hey[40] and Bristol Royal Infirmary[41] scandals. However, just as the circumstances of the medical profession of 1815 were determined by the actions

32 Ibid.: 69.

33 JA Simpson and ESC Weiner, editors, *The Oxford English Dictionary*, 2nd ed., Vol. 1 (Oxford: Oxford University Press, [1989] 1991) 807.

34 Christian Kay, Jane Roberts, Michael Samuels and Irené Wotherspoon, editors, *Historical Thesaurus of the Oxford English Dictionary*, Vol. 1 (Oxford: Oxford University Press, 2009) 147, 01.02.03.04.05/07., and also at: 1132, 02.05.01/04.

35 *See* note 29: 69.

36 Immanuel Kant, *Fundamental Principles of the Metaphysic of Morals*, 1785. In: Mortimer J Adler, editor, *Great Books of the Western World*, 2nd ed. (Chicago: Encyclopaedia Britannica Inc., [1952] 1990) 277.

37 *See* note 34: 1132, 02.05.01/00.

38 Robert Young, The implications of determinism. In: Peter Singer, editor, *A Companion to Ethics* (Oxford: Blackwell Publishing, 1991) 534–42.

39 *The Shipman Inquiry* (London: Stationery Office, 2002) (www.the-shipman-inquiry.org.uk/reports.asp, accessed: 22 June 2010).

40 *The Royal Liverpool Children's Inquiry Report* (London: Stationery Office, 2001) (www.rlcinquiry.org.uk, accessed: 22 June 2010).

41 *Learning from Bristol: the Report of the Public Inquiry into Children's Heart Surgery at the Bristol Royal Infirmary* (London: Stationery Office, 2001) (www.bristol-enquiry.org.uk, accessed: 22 June 2010).

of Henry V in trying to control the actions of the quacks of the 15th century, and in turn influenced the development and regulation of the modern-day general practitioner, so too will events of the late 20th century and early 21st century determine the degree of freedom of tomorrow's profession. The notion of self-regulation, albeit an intra-professional activity, has been heavily influenced by past events, both societal and legal. It has been a process that has fostered nothing more than an illusion of professional autonomy, for the autonomy of today's medical practitioners has, in fact, been mortgaged by our medical forefathers. For example, Cronin, in his novel *The Citadel*,[42] published in 1937, wrote about what he saw within the medical profession as 'its injustices, its hide-bound unscientific stubbornness, its humbug',[43] something he had to later publicly justify.[44] *The Citadel* subsequently became a book that was recognised as laying the foundations of the National Health Service in 1948;[45] particularly in Scotland.[46] Whilst Bevan[47] tried to allay the fears of the medical profession, stating that he would vigilantly watch 'that your own intellectual and scientific freedom is never at risk of impairment',[48] some doctors were not convinced,[49] recognising that 'State control of the profession is no new venture'.[50] Despite Bevan's reassurances, the freedoms and controls of the medical profession in 2010 were as much determined by the enactments of 1946–8 as today's process of revalidation[51] will influence the freedom of tomorrow's doctors.

42 AJ Cronin, *The Citadel* (London: Victor Gollancz, 1937).
43 James Agate, Demolition on Harley Street (London: *Daily Express*) 1937, 2 Aug, 8.
44 AJ Cronin, Response to James Agate's article (London: *Daily Express,*) 1937, 5 Aug, 6.
45 National Health Services Act 1946.
46 *Birth of NHS in Scotland: An Expectant Public* (NHS Scotland, Scottish Government) (www.60yearsofnhsscotland.co.uk/history/birth-of-nhs-scotland/an-expectant-public.html, accessed: 22 June 2010).
47 Aneurin Bevan (1897–1960), Minister of Health 1945–51.
48 Aneurin Bevan, A message to the medical profession from the Minister of Health, *BMJ*, 1948; 2: 1.
49 Editorial, Retrospect and prospect, *BMJ*, 1948; 2: 30–1.
50 Lionel Whitby, The changing face of medicine, *BMJ*, 1948; 2: 2–6.
51 Secretary of State for Health, *Trust, Assurance, Safety – The Regulation of Health Professionals in the 21st Century* (London: The Stationery Office, 2007).

In the purest of philosophical terms, at no single time in history have doctors truly been able to exercise free will in shaping their professional standing and regulation; at best, they have merely been participants in the process of instigating social and legal control. That said, it is interesting to note that for some doctors such fettering was not seen as a hindrance, with the role of medical laws and ethics being seen as 'not so much to restrict the doctor as to offer a promise to the patient',[52] a medical echo, perhaps, of Sartre's adage that 'freedom is what you do with what's been done to you'.[53]

CONCLUSION

The relationship between doctors and society is a symbiotic one; the former have no raison d'être without the latter, and the latter needs healthcare to assist in maintaining the integrity of its structured whole. Therefore, it follows that doctors cannot be comprehensively autonomous, as they are irretrievably woven into the fabric of the society in which they function. That fabric is something which the society itself weaves, utilising the thread of law to unite the various components into a coherent functional whole. Any perception of freedom is thus only of a relative nature and operates in accordance with the general will of the society. It may therefore be concluded that, at a philosophical level, the law fetters doctors by default from the moment they signal their intention to practise. However, such socio-legal bindings are, for the reasons given above, of a harmonious and self-fulfilling nature.

52 John Berger, *A Fortunate Man: the story of a country doctor* (New York: Vintage, [1967] 1997) 68.
53 Jean-Paul Sartre, *No Exit and Three Other Plays* (New York: Vintage International, 1989).

Chapter 3

Medicine, law and society

'A potent quack, long versed in human ills,
Who first insults the victim whom he kills;
Whose murd'rous hand a drowsy bench protect,
And whose most tender mercy is neglect.'[1]

***The Village*, George Crabbe**

THE RELATIONSHIP BETWEEN SOCIETY, THE LAW AND THE MEDICAL profession is a complex association,[2] with each intricately entwined with the other two; although, notwithstanding the fact that 'medical law' has been recognised as a subject since 1788,[3] the unifying term 'medico-legal' did not enter the English language[4] until 1835.[5] Despite Hemingway's rather jaundiced view of the two professions ('writers should stick together like doctors and lawyers and wolves'),[6]

---

1 George Crabbe, *The Village* (1783) Bk I, l: 282. In: Stephen Derry, editor, *George Crabbe* (London: Phoenix, 1999) 8.
2 George J Annas, The art of medicine: doctors and lawyers and wolves, *Lancet*, 2008; 371: 1833.
3 *See* note 34, Vol. 1, 03.04.13.03/26.
4 JA Simpson and ESC Weiner, editors, *The Oxford English Dictionary*, 2nd ed., Vol. 9 (Oxford: Oxford University Press, 1989) 551.
5 John Forbes, Alexander Tweedie and John Conolly, editors, *The Cyclopaedia of Practical Medicine*, Vol. 4 (London: Sherwood, Gilbert and Piper, 1835) 558.
6 Carlos Baker, editor, *Ernest Hemingway: selected letters 1917–1961* (New York, Scribner Book Company, 2003).

the truth is that society cannot exist without laws;[7] law provides the fundamental agreements which form a country's constitution (whether written or unwritten as such).[8] As part of its 'social cohesion' role,[9] the law dictates how every facet of medicine is practised.[10] In the 21st century, the latter extends even to the type of clothes worn in hospitals (short sleeves, no ties or watches), which many see as without evidence but 'as a weapon in the campaign to de-professionalise medicine'.[11] Meanwhile, various advances in medical science result in medical practice pushing against legal boundaries (e.g. in the fields of cloning,[12] transplantation,[13] genetic testing[14] and euthanasia[15]) and thereby often influencing changes within the law[16] (with echoes in European Law,[17] individual jurisdictions such as Australia,[18] Germany[19] and the Netherlands[20]). Although law's

7 Raymond Wacks, *Law: a very short introduction* (Oxford: Oxford University Press, 2008) 20–1.

8 Anthony King, *The British Constitution* (Oxford: Oxford University Press, 2007) 3.

9 Raymond Wacks, *Philosophy of Law: a very short introduction* (Oxford: Oxford University Press, 2006) 76.

10 Margaret Brazier and Emma Cave, *Medicine, Patients and the Law*, 4th ed. (London: Penguin, [1987] 2007) vii.

11 Adrian Crisp, Letters to the Editor (London: *The Daily Telegraph*) 2010, 2 July: 25.

12 Additional Protocol to the Convention for the Protection of Human Rights and the Dignity of the Human Being with regard to the Application of Biology and Medicine, on the Prohibition of Cloning Human Beings 1998.

13 Additional Protocol to the Convention for the Protection of Human Rights and Biomedicine concerning Transplantation of Organs and Tissues of Human Origin 2002.

14 Additional Protocol to the Convention for the Protection of Human Rights and Biomedicine concerning Genetic Testing for Health Purposes 2008.

15 *R (on the application of Pretty) v DPP* [2001] UKHL 61; a case which attracted much public attention and made Diane Pretty the subject of considerable public sympathy: *Diane Pretty Dies*, BBC News, Sunday, 12 May 2002 (http://news.bbc.co.uk/1/hi/health/1983457.stm, accessed: 8 July 2010).

16 Michael Davies, *Medical Law*, 2nd ed. (Oxford: Oxford University Press, [1996] 1998) 1–4.

17 Convention for the Protection of Human Rights and Dignity of the Human Being with regard to the Application of Biology and Medicine: Convention on Human Rights and Biomedicine 1997.

18 Rights of the Terminally Ill Act 1995 (Australia).

19 *German court legalises euthanasia with patient consent*, BBC News, 25 June 2010 (http://news.bbc.co.uk/1/hi/world/europe/10414647.stm, accessed: 8 July 2010).

20 Termination of Life on Request and Assisted Suicide (Review Procedures) Act 2002 (Netherlands).

'pervasive influence'[21] on the medical profession and the practice of medicine is frequently viewed with 'exasperation and lamentation'[22] (with law being cast as a 'meddlesome intruder'[23] or even an 'insatiable cormorant'[24]), it is without question that 'no profession is above the law'.[25] However, it is not always in the best interest of society for medical professionals to practise defensively.[26] In short, the land between medicine and law might be better thought of as 'common ground' rather than 'battleground'. With both law and medicine effectively sanctioned by and answerable to society, law becomes what Teff called a 'phantom enemy' to medicine.[27]

Paradoxically, although one aspect of this book is to consider whether or not the law acts as medicine's nemesis, that very issue cannot easily be separated from the accusation that modern medicine itself is seen by some as society's nemesis.[28] According to Illich, 'The medical establishment has become a major threat to health'.[29] He argues that the issue should be dealt with by political means, with greater control over the way in which doctors influence the management of the nation's health.[30] Legal limits on the 'professional monopoly of physicians'[31] is Illich's answer to the problem. He cites the 1973 Public Law 92-603 of the United States of America (under which the medical profession was obliged to formulate protocols for the treatment of various illnesses) as an example of how the law can be slanted to serve the interests of the medical profession

21 Ben A Rich, *Strange Bedfellows: how medical jurisprudence has influenced medical ethics and medical practice* (New York: Kluwer Academic, 2001) vii.
22 Ibid.
23 Harvey Teff, *Reasonable Care* (Oxford: Clarendon Press, 1994) 3.
24 P Rhodes, Letter to the Editor, *The Times*, 12 May 1987.
25 *Hajgato v London Health Assn* [1982] 36 OR 2d 669.
26 *See* note 23: 15.
27 Ibid.: 4.
28 Ivan Illich, *Limits to Medicine. Medical Nemesis: the expropriation of health* (London: Marion Boyars Publishing, [1995] 2002).
29 Ibid.: v.
30 Ibid.: 10.
31 Ibid.: 35.

more so than the society it was purporting to assist.[32] In Illich's view, 'Medicine retains unchecked autonomy in defining what constitutes sickness'.[33] Illich is not alone with such views. In 1975, the World Health Organization (WHO) supported the idea that 'the deprofessionalisation of primary care'[34] was the most important process required in order to raise the general standards of health. The question as to whether that statement is true or not is bound up with what it is that defines a 'profession' or 'being a professional'.

However, what constitutes a 'profession' is not defined by statute.[35] The *Oxford Dictionary* defines 'profession' as: 'a paid occupation, especially one involving training and a formal qualification'.[36] The same source defines 'professional' as: 'relating or belonging to a profession; engaged in an activity as a paid occupation rather than as an amateur'.[37] The question therefore arises as to whether someone (the professional) or something (a profession) can be truly considered to exist in an autonomous state if the very identity of the subject is so ill-defined. Here, recourse to the common law provides a possible solution. In *IRC v Maxse*[38] Scrutton LJ held that: 'A profession involves the idea of an occupation requiring either purely intellectual skill, or if any manual skill as in . . . surgery, skill controlled by the intellectual skill of the operator . . .'.[39] A similar approach is followed by Allsop and Saks (2002) in defining the 'health professions',[40] although it is interesting that the government avoided the whole issue of defining the subject when it set out its process for regulating the

32 Ibid.: 235.
33 Ibid.: 116.
34 Ibid.: 227, and Kenneth W Newell, editor, *Health by the People* (Geneva: World Health Organization, 1975).
35 Elizabeth A Martin and Jonathan Law, editors, *Oxford Dictionary of Law*, 6th ed. (Oxford: Oxford University Press, [1983] 2006) 416.
36 Catherine Soanes, editor, *Compact Oxford English Dictionary*, 2nd ed. (Oxford: Oxford University Press, 2000) 903.
37 Ibid.
38 *IRC v Maxse* [1919] 1 KB 647.
39 Ibid.
40 Judith Allsop and Mike Saks, *Regulating the Health Professions* (London: Sage Publications, 2002) 4.

'health professionals' in 2007;[41] that said, theorists might class this as a political move, with the government being mindful of George Bernard Shaw's view that 'all professions are conspiracies against the laity'.[42]

As will be shown in later chapters, a process was commenced in Tudor times to regulate the practising of medicine. Gradually, the untrained person was sidelined in favour of the professional practitioner; a process often petitioned for by the qualified practitioners themselves, and one which was periodically given legitimacy by statute. Some authors argue that, despite the activities of Henry V and Henry VIII,[43] medicine only became truly professionalised in the 19th century with the 'rise of professional society'.[44] Porter is of the opinion that 'the Victorian state provided the medical profession with a mandate to self-police practice, qualification, and education'.[45] This encapsulates what Larson (1977) called 'social closure'[46] by the medical profession; a 'regulatory bargain'[47] that is underpinned by statute. In this respect, the law may be seen as 'medicine's friend', as it legitimised the professional recognition fought for since Tudor times, and, in the process, 'anointed' the profession with society's gift of autonomy.

The 18th century saw this process come to maturity in so far as the medical profession was then as close to absolute autonomy as it

41 Department of Health, *Trust, Assurance and Safety – The Regulation of the Health Professionals in the 21st Century* (London: The Stationery Office, 2007).

42 George Bernard Shaw [1906], *The Doctor's Dilemma* (Fairfield, IA: 1st World Library Literary Society, 2004) 29.

43 JT Hughes, *The Licensing of Medical Practitioners in Tudor England: legislation enacted by Henry VIII* (Vesalius, 2006) XII(I) 4.

44 Dorothy Porter, Medicine and industrial society: reform, improvement, and professionalization, *Victorian Studies*, 1993; 37(1): 137. See also: George Clark, The history of the medical profession: aims and methods, *Medical History*, 1966; 10: 213–20; and also: Harold Perkin, *The Third Revolution. Professional Elites in the Modern World* (London: Routledge, 1996) 6.

45 *See* note 44: 136.

46 Magali Sarfatti Larson, *The Rise of Professionalism: a sociological analysis* (London: University of California Press, 1977) 19–40.

47 Judith Allsop and Mike Saks, *Regulating the Health Professions* (London: Sage Publications, 2002) 4.

has probably ever been. The irony is that since then, and particularly towards the end of the 20th century, part of that process has been politically unwound at society's insistence;[48] a process in which the law has, by default, played a central role.[49] The latter, however, is not a new phenomenon. In 1835, Tocqueville wrote: 'There is hardly a political question . . . which does not sooner or later turn into a judicial one'.[50] Although he was primarily speaking of the USA, there is no doubt that yesterday's American trends tend to become today's British reality. Medico-legal disputes are no longer confined to the courtroom, and as a result 'courts have created additional turmoil within the wider society'.[51] (Examples of such conflicting turmoil are the public debates which ensued following *Burke*,[52] *Miss B.*[53] and *Pretty*.[54]) However, society in turn has also increasingly taken its medical disputes into the courtroom, to the point that medical litigation has risen faster than any other area of tort litigation.[55] In the words of Ham and Alberti, 'the old implicit compact between doctors . . . and society has broken'.[56] In Britain, this has been reflected in the rise of negligence claims (estimated as a 125-fold increase between 1977

48 Mary Ann Elston, The politics of professional power: medicine in a changing health service. In: Jonathan Gabe, Michael Calnan and Michael Bury, editors, *The Sociology of the Health Service* (New York: Routledge, 1991): 58–88.

49 E.g. see *Gillick v West Norfolk and Wisbech Area Health Authority and the DHSS* [1986] AC 112.

50 Alexis de Tocqueville, *Democracy in America* (New York: AS Barnes & Co., [1835] 1838) 270.

51 Elizabeth A. Cawthon, *Medicine on Trial: a sourcebook with cases* (California: ABC-CLIO Inc., 2004) xiv.

52 *Burke v GMC* [2005] EWCA Civ 1003. Reported in: *Patient loses right-to-food case*, BBC News, 28 July 2005 (http://news.bbc.co.uk/1/hi/health/4721061.stm, accessed: 10 July 2010).

53 *Re B (Adult: Refusal of Medical Treatment)* [2002] All ER 449. Reported in: Anna Whitney, A dogged legal fight to find a peaceful end, *The Independent*, London, Tuesday, 30 April 2002. And: KM Boyd, Was society's response adequate in the cases of Mrs Pretty and Ms B.? *J Med Ethics*, 2002; 28: 211–12.

54 *R. (on the application of Pretty) v DPP* [2001] UKHL 61. Reported in: Robert Verkaik, Diane Pretty loses case, while Miss B 'dies with dignity', *The Independent*, London, 30 April 2002.

55 Peter Cane in: Vivienne Harpwood, *Medicine, Malpractice and Misapprehensions* (Oxford: Routledge-Cavendish, 2007) 2.

56 Chris Ham and KGMM Alberti, The medical profession, the public, and the government, *BMJ*, 2002; 324: 838.

and 2005),[57] contributing to a call for judicial reform,[58] less medical autonomy and greater regulation,[59] with a concomitant drive to regulate even further those practitioners of ancillary, complementary and alternative forms of healthcare services.[60]

The legal process started by Henry VIII has never been so busy in this respect as it has been in the late 20th and early 21st centuries. However, the same legal process would appear to have turned from being a process working on behalf of a disparate and fledgling medical profession on behalf of a vulnerable society, to one manipulated by an empowered society against a now beleaguered medical profession, perceived to be excessively autonomous (a charge recognised by Irvine in respect to the failures of the GMC)[61] and no longer working purely for the best interests of society. In all cases, the law has been the tool to achieve the aim; in the first instance a friend of medicine[62] (and witnessing the judgments of Lord Denning in *Hatcher*,[63] *Roe*,[64] *Hucks*[65] and *Whitehouse*,[66] when he said: 'We must say, and say firmly, that, in a professional man, an error of judgement is not negligent'[67]) but, latterly, more of its nemesis; witness: 'The near infallibility of clinical judgement once propounded by Lord Denning is a thing of the past;'[68] and: 'medical professionals fall into no "special category" which singles them out for privileged treatment'.[69]

57 Peter Cane, *Atiyah's Accidents, Compensation and the Law*, 7th ed. (Cambridge: Cambridge University Press, 2006) 221.

58 Lord Woolf, 'Medical Negligence' in: *Access to Justice*, Section 4 (London: HMSO, 1996) IV: 15.

59 Liam Donaldson, *Good Doctors, Safer Patients* (London: Department of Health, 2006).

60 *The Regulation of the Non-Medical Healthcare Professions* (The Foster Review), (London: Department of Health, 2006).

61 Donald Irving, A short history of the General Medical Council, *Med Educ*, 2006; 40: 202–11.

62 *Bolam v Friern Hospital Management Committee* [1957] 1 WLR 582.

63 *Hatcher v Black* [1954] The Times, 2 July 1954.

64 *Roe v Ministry of Health* [1954] 2 QB 66.

65 *Hucks v Cole* [1968] 118 NLJ 469.

66 *Whitehouse v Jordan* [1981] 1 All ER 267, HL.

67 Ibid.

68 Margaret Brazier, Patient autonomy and consent to treatment: the role of the law? *Leg Stud*, 1987; 169: 170.

69 Dieter Giesen, *International Medical Malpractice Law* (Massachusetts: Kluwer Academic

In an increasingly secular society, and in consideration to the autonomy of the medical profession, it is perhaps a case of 'what the law giveth, the law taketh away'[70] – a biblical concept that still resonates.[71] Perhaps, applying Mill's liberalist view that individuals are in the best position to decide what is in their best interests, Simpson *et al.* (1991)[72] were correct in their assertion that what society is looking for is a 'collaborative autonomy',[73] a term which broadly translates into what is now better known as 'informed consent'.[74]

The gradual erosion of the medical profession's autonomous status may, in part, be due to the ready availability of information to the general public. Once the preserve of those who had undertaken prolonged periods of study and training, the knowledge base is now available through many resources, predominantly the internet. The question may well be asked as to whether today's society still needs professionals, or are professionals an anachronism in the 21st century? Indeed, there are some who perceive a public campaign to deprofessionalise medicine.[75] What is not readily available to the layperson in society (i.e. on a self-help basis) is the element of expertise to make sense of the plethora of information. That is where expertise is important, an area where the professional may still retain the dominant hand, assuming, that is, that society trusts the professional in that respect.[76] Here, the complex regulation of professionals through numerous ethical codes (in respect to confidentiality,[77] consent,[78]

Publishers, 1988) 93.

70 Job 1, v. 21, The Holy Bible, Authorised King James Version: 'the Lord gave, and the Lord hath taken away'.

71 Lord Woolf, Are the courts excessively deferential to the medical profession? *Med Law Rev*, 2001, 9(1): 1–16.

72 Michael Simpson *et al.*, Doctor-patient communication: the Toronto consensus statement, *BMJ*, 1991; 303: 1386.

73 *See* note 23: 196–229.

74 *See* the judgment of Lord Scarman in *Sidaway v Board of Governors of the Bethlem Royal Hospital and the Maudsley Hospital* [1985] AC 871, 883.

75 Adrian Crisp, Letters to the Editor, *The Daily Telegraph*, London, 2 July 2010, 25.

76 Judith Allsop and Mike Saks, *Regulating the Health Professions* (London: Sage Publications, 2002) 6.

77 General Medical Council, *Confidentiality* (London: GMC, 2009).

78 General Medical Council, *Consent: patients and doctors making decision together* (London:

infertility and embryology,[79] withdrawing treatment,[80] conflicts of interest,[81] research,[82] and doctor–patient relationships[83]) and disciplinary codes[84] may be a key factor in meeting that demand. (Indeed, the first introductory line of *Good Medical Practice*, the code of conduct for medical practitioners, speaks twice of the need for society to trust doctors.)[85] The National Clinical Assessment Service (NCAS), a body charged with working with doctors where there is concern over a doctor's performance, neatly encapsulates the modern concept of what professionalism is about: 'professionalism covers everything that patients and society expects of their health professionals, and for which professionals are personally accountable'.[86] In other words, in the 21st century, professionals are what society says they are, not what professionals self-decree. The best that professionals can do is to try to stay one step ahead by ensuring that the various codes of conduct and ethical codes underpinning the medical profession's activities are well regulated. If the profession is no longer to be in charge of formulating its own regulations, the policing of that regulation is, perhaps, the last bastion of professional autonomy. However, that too is being eroded. A diminished role for the General Medical Council in setting the standards of entry to the profession (through its loss of control over undergraduate medical education), the imposition of an independent tribunal to examine the most serious cases of fitness to practice, and the loss of elected representation on the GMC[87] all

GMC, 2008).

79 General Medical Council, *Human Fertilisation and Embryology Authority Code of Practice*, 8th ed. (London: GMC, 2004).

80 General Medical Council, *Withholding and Withdrawing Life-Prolonging Treatments: good practice in decision-making* (London: GMC, 2002).

81 General Medical Council, *Conflicts of Interest* (London: GMC, 2008).

82 General Medical Council, *Research: the role and responsibilities of doctors* (London: GMC, 2002).

83 General Medical Council, *Maintaining Boundaries* (London: GMC, 2006).

84 General Medical Council, *Good Medical Practice* (London: GMC, 2006).

85 Ibid.: i.

86 National Clinical Assessment Agency, *Professionalism – dilemmas and lapses* (NHS National Patient Safety Agency, 2009) 2.

87 Fiona Godlee, Concerns about revalidation, *BMJ*, 2006; 333: 966.

serve to undermine the foundations of autonomous professionalism. Contemporary society has, at its centre, the need for professional expertise. However, as Johnson points out, leaders need a sense of destiny, and therefore the demoralisation of professionals which is inevitably concomitant with loss of control is not necessarily in society's best interests.[88] However, 'professional society is an elusive concept with a hazy chronology'.[89] If both are to survive, society and the medical profession both need the redrawing of the contract between the two;[90] the law is perhaps the natural mediator to facilitate this process.[91]

CONCLUSION

The philosophical interaction between medicine, law and society has already been discussed in Chapter 1. In this chapter, that earlier discussion has been furthered, with a reflection on how pervasive the law is in respect to determining the parameters by which a doctor is permitted to function within English society. In this respect, the law is both permissive and constraining, as though saying 'you may . . . but only if, or by, or in accordance with'. In this respect, the law has a duality: it is both friend and foe, libertarian and adjudicator.

However, it would seem that there is a paradox. By allowing the medical profession the freedom to exist and function, the law might be inadvertently acting as a nemesis to the very society which it serves. On the other hand, by regulating the role of doctors and limiting their autonomy on behalf of society, the law assumes an adversarial relationship to medicine. The balance between these dichotomies appears to be found within the concept of professionalism, wherein

88 James Johnson, Independence is key to better regulation, *BMJ*, 2006; 333: 966–7.

89 Michael Thompson, *Reviews in History: the third revolution. Professional elites in the modern world* (London: The Institute of Historical Research, 1997), 29 (www.history.ac.uk/reviews/review/29#t9, accessed: 6 July 2010).

90 William M Sullivan, Medicine under threat: professionalism and professional identity, *CMAJ*, 2000; 162(5): 673.

91 *See* note 23: 239.

there is the relative freedom for a degree of self-regulation within predetermined socio-legal boundaries, boundaries which are in turn continuously being reshaped by society through the fluid medium of the common law.

Chapter 4

The ancients' perspective of medicine

Doctors and the law from 400 BCE to 1700 CE

'Medicine is of all the Arts the most noble; but, owing to the ignorance of those who practise it, and of those who, inconsiderately, form a judgment of them, it is at present far behind all the other arts. Their mistake appears to me to arise principally from this, that in the cities there is no punishment connected with the practice of medicine (and with it alone) except disgrace, and that does not hurt those who are familiar with it. Such persons are like the figures which are introduced in tragedies, for as they have the shape, and dress, and personal appearance of an actor, but are not actors, so also physicians are many in title but very few in reality.'[1]

Hippocrates (400 BCE)

1 Hippocrates (400 BCE). In: Francis Adams, translator, *The Genuine Works of Hippocrates translated from the Greek* [Sydenham Society, 1849], (Florida, Krieger Publishing Company, 1972).

HISTORY INFORMS THE PRESENT, AND WITH DILIGENT USE OF THE lessons learned, it should be possible to influence the future in a positive way. Whitby (1948)[2] reminds us that Churchill certainly recognised this when he stated: 'The longer you can look back the farther you can look forward.'[3] Orwell took a more jaundiced view.[4] Nonetheless, looking back to the 4th century BCE we know that Hippocrates[5] recognised the need to regulate physicians and the practice of medicine (as noted above). However, he was a man before his time, as it has really only been in the late 20th century that patients' legal rights have started to bring the law in conflict with the ethical principles of the medical profession.[6] This may partially be due to the shaky foundation upon which the practice of medicine was built in ancient times. If Aristotle,[7] a near contemporary (in historical terms) of Hippocrates, is considered as the 'last person to know everything there was to be known in his own time'[8] and most of his views on medicine have been superseded by later discoveries, it is easier to see how Hippocrates' desire to control the practice of medicine fell at the first hurdle. Nonetheless, his Hippocratic Oath[9] has lasted as a basis upon which modern codes of conduct are based.[10]

Galen[11] followed Hippocrates as one of history's most notable physicians. However, if modern day clinicians feel restricted by laws such

---

2 Lionel Whitby, The changing face of medicine, *BMJ*, 1948; 2: 2.

3 Winston Churchill, A speech in proposing the toast of the College at the Luncheon of The Royal College of Physicians in London, 2 March 1944. In: Winston S Churchill, *The Dawn of Liberation* (London: Cassell, 1944) 21–5.

4 'He who controls the past, controls the future; who controls the present, controls the past'. George Orwell, *1984* (St Louis, MO: Turtleback Books, [1948] 1999) 248.

5 Hippocrates (460–377 BCE), Greek physician.

6 Lars Fallberg, Do doctors know about their legal responsibilities? *Eur J Health Law*, 2006; 13: 91.

7 Aristotle (384–322 BCE), a Greek philosopher and writer.

8 Alex Neill and Aaron Ridley, *The Philosophy of Art: readings ancient and modern* (Maidenhead: McGraw-Hill, 1995) 488.

9 Veronica English, Gillian Romano-Critchley, Julian Sheather and Ann Sommerville, *Medical Ethics Today*, 2nd ed. (London: BMJ Books, [1993] 2004) 770.

10 Felix Marti-Ibanez, *A Prelude to Medical History* (New York: MD Publications, 1961) 86.

11 Galen (129–199 BCE), a Greek physician and philosopher.

as the Human Tissue Act 2004,[12] Galen worked under even greater regulation, as the Roman law of 150 BCE prohibited the dissection of human cadavers.[13] Such knowledge lends credence to the suspicion that medicine has never been a truly autonomous profession, and that the law has acted as a governor in certain areas of practice since ancient Greek and Roman times.

Prior to Hippocrates, and the advent of scientific medicine, laws regarding health and the practice of healing rituals were largely laid down within religious texts, which is not surprising considering that priests were also the physicians of the day. The Book of Leviticus[14] is a prime example.[15] Ancient Persia also legislated to control the practice of medicine. A professional code, specifying training requirements and outlining fees and penalties for malpractice, is included within the Vendidad.[16] Furthermore, evidence of even greater control is available from far earlier eras. The Code of Hammurabi,[17] attributed to King Hammurabi (1948–1905 BCE), first defined the concept of physicians' civil and criminal liabilities in respect to the Assyrian and Babylonian civilisations.[18]

In England, particularly during the Dark Ages[19] after the demise of the Roman Empire, very little progress was made in the field of regulating the practice of medicine until the reign of King Henry V. Even then, legislation did not materialise until the reign of Henry VIII.[20]

12 Part 1 of the Human Tissue Act 2004 provides the law for the 'Removal, Storage and Use of Human Organs and Other Tissue for Scheduled Purposes', whilst Part 2 describes the 'Regulation of Activities Involving Human Tissue'.

13 Arthur C Aufderheide, *The Scientific Study of Mummies* (Cambridge: Cambridge University Press, 2003) 5.

14 Written c. 550–400 BCE, the Book of Leviticus is the third book of the Hebrew Bible, and was later incorporated into the Jewish Torah.

15 Leviticus verses 11–16 lays down the laws in respect to cleanliness, health, leprosy, circumcision, and the treatment of bodily discharges such as blood, semen and pus.

16 Unknown author, *The Zend Avesta, Part 1 of 3: The Vendidad* (Forgotten Books, 2008).

17 The *Codex Hammurabi* (c. 1790 BCE) is on display in the Louvre, Paris.

18 LW King (Translator), *The Code of Hammurabi* (Sioux Falls, SD: NuVision Publications, [1915] 2007).

19 The period otherwise known as the 'Middle Ages', between the fall of the Roman Empire in the West (476 CE) and the Renaissance (14th century CE).

20 JT Hughes, *The Licensing of Medical Practitioners in Tudor England: legislation enacted by*

Up until then, although there were some doctors who held medical degrees, the public were largely dependent upon 'medical skills offered by surgeons, apothecaries and various quacks, empirics and mountebanks'.[21] It was the universities of Oxford and Cambridge who, in 1421, first called for legislation to restrict the ability to practise medicine to their graduates.[22] Although it may be argued that this was a protectionist move on behalf of the qualified physicians, and one of the earliest examples of restrictive practice, Henry V saw it as a means of protecting the innocent poor. As a result, the Lords of the King's Council were given powers to punish unqualified practitioners.[23]

Henry VIII followed through with no less than seven Acts of Parliament[24] designed to regulate the practice of medicine and surgery, and to discourage unqualified practitioners.[25] The first,[26] passed in 1512/1513,[27] made it necessary to obtain a licence from the Bishop of London or the Dean of St Paul's Cathedral before practising as a physician or surgeon in London; outside of London, a licence had to be obtained from the Bishop of the relevant diocese.[28] One year later, a second Act[29] exempted barber surgeons from wearing armour.[30] In 1523, an Act[31] gave power to the College of Physicians of London to examine and appoint all physicians throughout the country.[32]

Henry VIII (Vesalius, 2006) XII(I) 4.

21 Andrzej Kuropatnicki, English Medicine in the Tudor Times, *Archiwum historii i filozofil medycyny*, 2003, 66(2): 109–17.

22 *See* note 20.

23 Rotuli Parliamentorum, IV, 130. In: C Given-Wilson, editor, *The Parliament Rolls of Medieval England, 1275–1504* (Leicester: Scholarly Digital Editions, 2005).

24 The seven Acts can be found in *The Statutes of the Realm*, printed by Command of King George III (London: The Record Commission, 1817).

25 *See* note 20: 6–8.

26 An Act concerning Physicians & Surgeons, An. 3 Henry VIII c. 11 (1512/1513).

27 In the reign of Henry VIII, the year 1512 ended on 24 March. Using a modern calendar, the year would be 1513.

28 *Statutes of the Realm* (London, 1817), 3: 31–2.

29 An Act that Surgeons be discharged of Constableshipe & other things, An. 5 Henry VIII c. 6 (1513/1514).

30 *Statutes of the Realm* (London, 1817), 3: 95.

31 An Act concerning Physicians, An. 14 Henry VIII c. 15 (1523).

32 *Statutes of the Realm* (London, 1817), 3: 213–14.

Surgeons were given extra protection against immigrant practitioners[33] in 1530/1531,[34] whilst the physicians had to wait until 1540[35] for the same privileges as that granted to the barber surgeons in 1513/1514, exempting them from certain civic duties. The same Act gave the physicians power to inspect the apothecaries' warehouses, and to legally practise surgery as well as medicine;[36] whereas the surgeons were not legally allowed to practise medicine.

The final two Acts under Henry VIII related to surgeons. In 1540, an Act[37] was passed which amalgamated the surgeons and barber surgeons into one company, exempted the surgeons from bearing arms, encouraged the teaching of anatomy, and restricted the barber surgeons to the drawing of teeth and external treatments only.[38] Two years later, a 1542 Act[39] made it legal for unqualified healers to administer 'external therapies', but only if no fee was charged.[40]

The aforementioned seven Acts of Henry VIII are worth noting, as they mark an important transition in legal history. Prior to the 16th century, there had been little control over the practice of medicine or surgery since the teachings of the ancient Greeks and a few edicts from Rome. However, although the Acts of Henry VIII started to bring about a degree of regulation, it is clear that, for the most part, the law was foremost designed to protect the standing of the physicians, with some secondary protection for the work of the surgeons and barber surgeons. The law did not make it easier for other trained therapists (such as the apothecaries) to assist those who could not afford the fees of the physicians, but kept them constrained, essentially as technicians to the physicians. Neither did the law work in favour of

33 Ibid.: 332.
34 An Act concerning Bakers, Brewers, Surgeons, and Scriveners, An. 22 Henry VIII c. 13 (1530/1531).
35 An Act Concerning Physicians, An. 32 Henry VIII c. 40 (1540).
36 *Statutes of the Realm* (London, 1817), 3: 793.
37 An Act Concerning Barbers and Surgeons, An. 32 Henry VIII c. 42 (1540).
38 *Statutes of the Realm* (London, 1817), 3: 794–6.
39 An Act that persons being not surgeons may minister medicines outwardly, An. 34 & 35 Henry VIII c. 8 (1542).
40 *Statutes of the Realm* (London, 1817), 3: 906.

the vulnerable public by directly outlawing the work of the abundant quacks and mountebanks.[41] However, for the physician, Tudor law went a long way towards sanctioning professional autonomy in respect to the regulation of entry into the profession, whilst providing no control over the actual standard of practice or the quality of the treatments offered; such matters were left to the physicians to determine for themselves. For the 16th-century surgeon, the law was less accommodating, although it did allow for certain privileges and restricted the role of the barber surgeons.

A passing point of interest is the fact that some of Henry VIII's Acts clashed with earlier ones. For example, the 1523 Act did not repeal the 1512/1513 Act, thereby presenting a legal clash between the rights and responsibilities of the physicians versus the bishops. Indeed, it is fascinating to note that, owing to the fact that the 1523 Act was unenforceable (due to the lack of influence of the College of Physicians outside London), the 1512/1513 Act was only really surpassed by the 1858 Medical Act[42] (*see* Chapter 5). Indeed, it was not until the National Health Service Act 1946 that the 1523 Act was formally repealed.[43]

Case law during the 16th and 17th centuries was equally protective of the physicians. For example, in 1606 in the judgment in *Dr Laughton v Gardener*[44] the plaintiff was fined five pounds for every month he 'used the art of physic in London, without licence from the college'.[45]

However, it was not always so. On occasions, the law worked against the physicians on technical grounds, despite evidence of unlicensed practising of medicine. In 1606, Dr Bonham was successful in his case against the College of Physicians for false imprisonment

---

41 Quacks worked from fixed addresses, whereas mountebanks were peripatetic.

42 The 1858 Medical Act's long title was 'an Act to regulate the Qualifications of Practitioners in Medicine and Surgery'.

43 *See* note 20: 7.

44 *Dr Laughton v Gardener* [1606] 79 ER 104.

45 Ibid.

despite having been found practising medicine without a licence.[46] The law again declared its impartiality in *The Corporation of Physitians v Doctor Tenant* for practising of physic,[47] the judgment was *quod querens nil capiat per billam*[48]on the grounds that the declaration had not been appropriately made in law and should thus be unsuccessful. A similar case was heard and found in favour of the plaintiff (Doctor Trigg) on appeal in 1652,[49] when it was found that the initial judgment given against Doctor Trigg should have been given in favour of the College of Physicians and the King, and not just in favour of the College.

Occasionally, a judgment was given which showed some consideration towards the plight of the poor, and accordingly against the physicians. In *College of Physicians v Butler*[50] Chief Justice Richardson upheld the 1512/1513 law of King Henry VIII, namely that: 'no man should practise physic in London, or within seven miles, without licence under the seal of the college'. However, the judgment also gave leeway for unqualified practitioners to administer herbal remedies, but only if they did so on charitable grounds and did not take a fee for their service, thereby outlawing unqualified practice for financial gain.[51] The judgment was confirmed on appeal.[52]

These aforementioned cases imply that the legal stance during the 17th century was to generally support the physicians in their quest to protect their income from the practice of medicine, but did little to regulate the actual quality of practice. As Pelling put it: 'in spite of the College's humanist programme, collegiate physicians did not

46 *Bonham's Case* [1606] 77 ER 646.
47 *The Corporation of Physitians v Doctor Tenant for practising of physic* [1613] 80 ER 1054.
48 That the plaintiff take nothing by his bill.
49 *Doctor Trigg v College of Physicians* [1652] 82 ER 751.
50 *College of Physicians v Butler* [1628] (6 Charles 1).
51 Editorial, The Proposed Amendment of the Penal Clauses of the Medical Acts, *BMJ*, 1894; 1: 921.
52 *Butler v The President of the College of Physicians* [1631] 79 ER 823.

frame their body's authority through their own writings: prosecution took precedence over publication . . .'.[53]

Indeed, the college's own records indicate that from 1550 to 1640 the college of physicians tried to restrict the practice of 714 unlicensed 'practitioners of physic'.[54] However, unlicensed practice was not in itself a criminal act,[55] and, as a result, the law was not unequivocally unkind towards the physicians, disallowing cases or overturning judgments where due legal process had not been correctly followed despite evidence of unlicensed medical practice (as noted above).

CONCLUSION

Whilst there is evidence for the legal control of the practice of medicine in some early civilisations, those laws were predominantly punitive, with poor practice being punished. The ancient Greeks were the first to introduce a Code of Practice, now known as the Hippocratic Oath. That code's essence has carried forward to modern day professional codes of practice. In England, Roman law did little to alter the legislation of medical practice apart from prohibiting the dissection of human cadavers, and the Dark Ages saw a return to unregulated quackery. It was not until the middle of the 16th century that the law was used to significantly influence medical practice in England, and only then to partially control unlicensed practitioners rather than regulate the standards of the qualified physicians. The latter had a high level of autonomy, utilising the law to protect their professional standing to a degree which must rank as one of the first examples of restrictive practices. For the 16th-century physician, the law was most certainly designed to meet the requirements of the medical profession. A study of case law reveals that this was a

53 Margaret Pelling, *Medical Conflicts in Early Modern London: patronage, physicians and irregular practitioners 1550–1640* (Oxford: Clarendon Press, 2003) 2.

54 *College of Physicians of London Database*, British History Online (www.british-history.ac.uk/report.aspx?compid=18021, accessed: 14 August 2010).

55 Ibid.

situation which continued well into the 17th century, with the main thrust being the control of unlicensed practitioners, particularly within London. Whilst entry into the ranks of the physicians was highly self-regulated, there is little evidence to show that the subsequent standard of practice of the physicians was regulated to any meaningful extent. For the licensed physician of the 16th and 17th centuries, the law was most certainly a friend.

Chapter 5

The evolution and legal recognition of the general medical practitioner

'Freedom is what you do with what's been done to you.'[1]

Jean-Paul Sartre, French Philosopher (1905–80)

A QUACK WAS, IN THE 18TH-CENTURY WORDS OF SAMUEL JOHNSON:[2]

1 A boastful pretender to arts which he does not understand.
2 A vain boastful pretender to physic; one who proclaims his own medical abilities in public places.
3 An artful tricking practitioner in physick;

whilst quackery was defined as: 'Mean or bad acts in physick'.[3] However, having seen in the previous chapter that quackery itself was not outlawed by 16th and 17th-century laws, there remains a degree of controversy as to exactly when the legal suppression of quackery commenced.

---

1 Jean-Paul Sartre, *No Exit and three other plays* (New York: Vintage International, 1989).
2 Samuel Johnson, *Johnson's Dictionary*, Vol. 2 (London: Knapton, Longman & Co., 1755).
3 Ibid.

King Henry VIII founded the Royal College of Physicians in 1518,[4] following their petition to be allowed to grant licences to men qualified in medicine; thus, in the words of Sir Winston Churchill, 'casting a stern Tudor frown upon quackery of all kinds'.[5] However, it is perhaps the case that Sir Winston was a little inaccurate in his history, as it was not until the Medical Act of 1858 that there was a real turning point in this respect.[6] In addition, the College of Physicians was not alone in being able to grant licences; the Archbishop of Canterbury had the right to issue licences to practitioners throughout the province of Canterbury (extending from 'England south of the Humber and the whole of Wales'),[7] under Peter's Pence Act 1533.[8] From the Directory of Medical Licences 1535–1775, held in the Lambeth Palace Library, it is clear that the Archbishop of Canterbury exercised this right with considerable frequency until the last dispensation was issued in 1775.[9]

Despite the above, and the fact that Henry VIII gave the physicians the ability to punish unlicensed practice, the 1700s saw the continuance of the work of those without qualifications; the practitioners who: 'had no medical degrees, diplomas or certificates; they were not enrolled in medical colleges or corporations, or licensed to practise'.[10]

4 Royal College of Physicians, *College History* (www.rcplondon.ac.uk/history-heritage/College-history-new/Pages/Overview.aspx, accessed: 28 June 2010).

5 Winston Churchill, A Speech in proposing the toast of the college at the luncheon of The Royal College of Physicians in London, 2 March 1944. In: Winston S Churchill, *The Dawn of Liberation* (London: Cassell, 1944) 21–5.

6 The Medical Registration Act 1858 made it such that a man employed by Union workhouses had to hold dual qualifications in medicine and surgery and be registered.

7 Lambeth Palace Library, *Lambeth Palace Library Research Guide: Medical Licences Issued by the Archbishop of Canterbury 1535–1775* (www.lambethpalacelibrary.org/files/Medical_Licences.pdf, accessed: 21 August 2010) 2.

8 Otherwise known as the Ecclesiastical Licences Act 1533, the Act outlawed Peter's Pence (a payment previously made by landowners to the Pope) and transferred to Canterbury the right to issue dispensations previously issued by the Pope.

9 Lambeth Palace Library, op. cit.: 3.

10 Roy Porter, *Quacks, Fakers and Charlatans in Medicine* (Stroud: Tempus Publishing, [1989] 2003) 18.

Many of these (470 recorded between the years 1500 to 1700)[11] were 'Hugenot refugee doctors'.[12]

Mehlman (2005) took the view that, in America, quacks materialised as an answer to the deficiencies of legitimate medical practices.[13] However, in England, the problem which faced those who sought to outlaw such activity was that, contrary to Johnson's view, many such practitioners did have a sound knowledge of medicine, despite their lack of qualification. A large number were, for example, apothecaries: tradesmen skilled in the art of preparing the medicines as prescribed by the licensed physicians, and who also frequently administered medicines to the poor without instruction from a physician.

This is a conundrum which has continued even to the modern day; the question being whether a quack is, as Johnson maintained in 1755 (noted p. 35), someone lacking knowledge or expounding false knowledge, or someone who knows what they are doing but is unlicensed to do it. Courts in other jurisdictions have had equal difficulty in lending clarification. In *McFadden v U.S. Fidelity and Guarantee Co*,[14] the court took the view that a quack was 'an *untrained* person who pretends to be a physician'[15] (my italics); whereas in *State v Hoffman*,[16] the court used the same definition to convict 'for the practice of medicine *without a licence*'[17] (my italics).

Stoking this controversial subject, an editorial in the *British Medical Journal* in 1900 offered the concept, which it called 'the nemesis of quackery': 'Quackery is in its effect opposite to mercy – it curses him that gives as well as him that takes.'[18] However, as Aronson (1997) asked when discussing how various accepted medical practices have

11 Leslie G Matthews, London's Immigrant Apothecaries, 1600–1800, *Med Hist*, 1974; 18: 262.
12 Ibid.
13 Maxwell J Mehlman, Quackery, *Am J Law Med*, 2005; 31: 350.
14 *McFadden v U.S. Fidelity and Guarantee Co* 766 So. 2d 20 (Miss. Ct. App. 2000).
15 *See* note 11: 355.
16 *State v Hoffman* 558 P.2d 602 (Utah 1976).
17 Ibid.
18 Editorial, The nemesis of quackery, *BMJ*, 1900; 1: 921.

subsequently been disproven and fallen into disrepute: 'who knows what modern views will be looked upon as quackish in 50 years time?'[19] This is the 'obsolete science' referred to by Clark (1966),[20] who recognised that, for the medical man of the 17th and 18th centuries, 'their light was darkness'.[21] The aforementioned is in tune with the sentiment of Hodgkin (1830), who understood that 'quackery ought to disappear, but it cannot be put down by law'.[22]

In keeping with the above, and despite the primary legislation of the Tudors, the early 18th century began to see case law developing in favour of the apothecaries. An example of this is the landmark case of *The College of Physicians v Rose*.[23] The physicians maintained that Rose (an apothecary who visited a sick person, made a judgment as to the nature of the condition and then provided medication to relieve the condition), was acting contrary to the statute of Henry VIII.[24] The court found in favour of the plaintiff. However, Rose appealed (by obtaining a writ of error from the Attorney General)[25] on the grounds that he only charged for the medicines, and had not, in so doing, practised as a physician or violated their privileges. As a result, the original judgment was reversed in the House of Lords, who disagreed with the *ratio decidendi* of the original judges.[26] It was a decision which was not contested until 1830.[27]

Rose was an important test case supported by the Society of Apothecaries.[28] Cases such as this marked a turning point in the

19 Jeff Aronson, When I use a word . . . quacks, *BMJ*, 1997; 315 (19 July).
20 George Clark, The history of the medical profession: aims and methods, *Medical History*, 1966; 10(3): 215.
21 Ibid.
22 In Roy Porter, *Quacks, Fakers and Charlatans in Medicine* (Stroud, Tempus Publishing, [1989] 2003) 54.
23 *The College of Physicians v Rose* [1703] 87 ER 806.
24 Statute 14 and 15 Hen. 8. C. 5.
25 Penelope Hunting, *A History of the Society of Apothecaries* (London: The Society of Apothecaries, 1998) 55.
26 *William Rose v The College of Physicians, London* [1703] 2 ER 857.
27 Irvine Loudon, *Medical Care and the General Medical Practitioner 1750–1850* (Oxford: Clarendon Press, 1986) 22.
28 Cecil Wall, *The London Apothecaries* (London: The Apothecaries Hall, c.1960) 5.

regulation of medical practice. No longer was the law simply a tool in the hands of the physicians to protect their privileges and to restrict medical practice to those with a medical qualification.[29] The common law was highlighting a need within society: a need which identified that the public needed protection against the unscrupulous, but also against the constraints of the 'medical oligarchy'[30] – a want which eventually led to the Apothecaries Act of 1815, thereby legislating for the first time for a branch of medicine today known as general practice.[31]

It is suggested that, for the philosopher considering medico-legal ethics, this entire process lends some considerable degree of ambiguity, if not forming an interesting paradox, especially when the four principles[32] of Beauchamp and Childress[33] are retrospectively applied. Of course, it may be argued that it is inappropriate to measure medico-legal activity of the 16th to 19th centuries though the application of 21st-century theories of biomedical ethics. However, there is something salutary in doing so, especially if the warnings of Aronson and Clark (noted on p. 38) are considered. The latter suggests a paradox, which is explained below.

A respect for autonomy is usually applied in respect to patients rather than to the medical profession itself. However, it is true to say that the 16th and 17th-century physicians (in particular) had considerable autonomy in so far as deciding on the manner in which they practised, tailor-making their treatments for the 'constitution and lifestyle' of the patient concerned.[34] Those known as quacks (the unqualified and unlicensed) had just as much, if not more, autonomy, as quackery in itself was not illegal and such practitioners were free to do as they willed as long as they did not fall foul of being

29 *See* note 25.
30 *See* note 10: 55.
31 Ibid.: 54.
32 The four principles are Respect for Autonomy, Non-maleficence, Beneficence and Justice.
33 Tom L Beauchamp and James F Childress, *Principles of Biomedical Ethics*, 6th ed. (Oxford: Oxford University Press, 2009) 99–240.
34 Andrew Wear, Historical keywords – quack, *Lancet*, 2005; 366: 1157.

accused of unlawfully acting as a physician. The apothecaries had far less autonomy, essentially being servants to the physicians. Patients also had less autonomy. The rich could choose the physician they wished to have treat them. However, the poor either had to contend with the quacks or hope that they could find a charitable apothecary who would risk treating them without a physician's authority. Any such benevolent behaviour by an apothecary risked being the subject of a law suit brought by the College of Physicians. As such action was to the detriment of those most in need, it far from epitomised the principle of justice.[35] So, in general, during the 17th and 18th centuries, those with the most autonomy (the physicians) exercised little benevolence; those who exercised the most benevolence (the apothecaries) had little autonomy and were subject to the malevolence of the physicians; those whose autonomy went largely unchecked, but who exercised the least benevolence, and whose actions were often far from being non-malevolent, were the quacks. Those most in need of benevolence (the poor sick) had the least autonomy, were often the subjects of the malevolence (directly by the quacks, and indirectly through the actions of the physicians against the apothecaries) and saw little in the way of justice.

Until the charter of King James I in 1617,[36] the apothecaries were not even autonomous in respect to their trade body,[37] and even then the law was weighted against them:

> At first they had a very low position,
> Kept shop while they dispensed for the physician
> And, though they learned a lot of useful knowledge,
> Were quite subdued by the Physicians' College
> Which had the right their drug-shops to inspect,
> To test their medicines and the bad reject.

35 *See* note 33: 240.
36 *See* note 25: 33.
37 Ibid.: 14–15. The apothecaries were formerly part of the association of Pepperers (1180) and subsequently, members of the Grocers' Company (1373).

Apothecaries could not patients treat,
Or, if they did, they had to be discreet,
For, if the College of Physicians heard,
The culprit suffered and a fine incurred.[38]

The *Rose* case (noted above) did much to reverse this situation in law, and the standing of the apothecaries was further enhanced in 1813 when a petition was presented to the House of Commons claiming that 'there is no existing law to prevent persons, without any proper medical education, from practising [as apothecaries, surgeon apothecaries or midwifery]'.[39] The result of the above was the Apothecaries Act 1815, the long title of which ('An Act for better regulating the Practice of Apothecaries throughout England and Wales') signalled the start of a new era of regulation of medical practice by imposing a legal requirement for a formal medical qualification and, in particular, set the scene for the modern general practitioner. It was also the closest the 19th century came to outlawing the unqualified and unregulated quacks who had heretofore abounded unchecked by the law, for the Act specifically stated that 'it shall not be lawful for any person . . . to practise as an apothecary . . . in any part of England or Wales, unless he . . . shall have been examined by, and received a certificate of his . . . being duly qualified to practise as such'.[40] Perhaps for the first time in recorded history, the law was on the side of the majority of the medical practitioners (as opposed to the members of the College of Physicians), as well as the general population who depended so much on the work of the apothecaries. However, the situation did not remain settled, and Hansard has recorded a series of parliamentary debates over the course of the next century which

38 Zachary Cope, from the poem: 'The Story of The Worshipful Society of Apothecaries'; *The Worshipful Society of Apothecaries of London and the Evolution of the Family Doctor* (London: The Society of Apothecaries, c. 1967) 11.

39 Hansard (London: United Kingdom Parliament) 1813, 19 Nov, Vol. 27: cols. 164–5.

40 An Account of the Origin of the Association of Apothecaries and Surgeon-Apothecaries, In: *Transactions of the Associated Apothecaries and Surgeon-Apothecaries of England and Wales*, Vol. 1 (London, 1823) xix.

reflect the troubled relationship between the various facets of the medical profession and the law, and it is not for nothing that the period 1794–1858 has been called 'The Period of Medical Reform'.[41]

For example, 1833 revealed difficulties with prescriptions being written in Latin and apothecaries not being able to read the same, with a subsequent (failed) attempt to repeal the Apothecaries Act;[42] 1834 saw a debate requesting that the a Select Committee be appointed 'to inquire into the laws and regulations, regarding the education and practice of the various branches of the medical profession, in the United Kingdom'.[43] February 1845 witnessed the debate being carried into the realms of the Poor Law Unions, with questions being raised in respect to the minimum qualifications demanded of 'medical officers' being appointed by the Boards of Guardians.[44] The same month had members of the Commons exercised over the monopoly of the College of Physicians, demanding new Charters for the Physicians and Surgeons of Dublin and Edinburgh,[45] whilst the controversial air of legal reform continued into May 1845, when it was considered 'indispensably necessary' to 'maintain the interests of the general practitioners' by incorporating them into a College of their own.[46] By 1851, the irony of this half-century of reform was complete: in a manner prescient of Sartre's later philosophical reflection on the issue of freedom (noted earlier), the apothecaries styled themselves 'general practitioners' and gradually distanced themselves from the preparation of medicines; 'chemists and druggists' filled the void, with the subsequent need to regulate the latter, an issue which resulted in the Pharmacy Bill of 1851.[47]

Finally, the Medical Act 1858 brought this flurry of reform to a

41 Irvine Loudon, *Medical Care and the General Medical Practitioner 1750–1850* (Oxford: Clarendon Press, 1986) 2.
42 Hansard (London: United Kingdom Parliament) 1833, 17 June, Vol. 18: cols. 912–13.
43 Hansard, 1834, 11 Feb, Vol. 21, cols. 233–6.
44 Hansard, 1845, 11 Feb, Vol. 77, cols. 298–304.
45 Hansard, 1845, 25 Feb, Vol. 77, cols. 1211–21.
46 Hansard, 1845, 7 May, Vol. 80, cols. 249–77.
47 Hansard, 1851, 2 July, Vol. 118, cols. 111–18.

close with the formation of the General Medical Council, requiring all medical practitioners to register with the Council and for the Council to supervise the training of doctors.

CONCLUSION

Having been left relatively undisturbed from the times of the ancient Greeks, with the exception of a fleeting interest from Henry VIII in the 16th century, the world of medicine had been largely left undisturbed by the law until the reforming years of the first part of the 19th century. It was then largely through primary legislation that the entire structure of the profession was reorganised and regulated. Unlike events during the 20th century (which will be discussed later), medico-legal case law (with the exception of the physicians suing for their fines for unlicensed practice) was in little evidence during this period, apart from the very important case of *William Rose v College of Physicians*.[48] Not only was the latter a legal turning point for the apothecaries, but it additionally illustrated how case law is important in the interpretation (and in this case, the reinterpretation) of primary legislation, especially when the latter had been enacted so long previously as to warrant its expounders to be accused of 'straining an act made so long ago'.[49]

For the physicians of 19th-century London, the law was most certainly its nemesis, as indeed it was for the many untrained quacks. However, for the emerging general practitioners (and indeed, for the good of the population) the law was most certainly used in a constructive and favourable manner. Such frenzied political attention would not be seen again until the formation of the NHS in 1948, and then again in the early 21st century (which is discussed in later chapters).

Not everyone was happy, however. Some historians see this era of

48 *William Rose v College of Physicians* [1703] 2 ER 857.
49 Ibid.: s. 554.

medico-legal reformation as a regressive step. Illich, for example, has difficulty with the progress medicine has made: 'By turning from art to science, the body of physicians has lost the traits of a guild of craftsmen applying rules established to guide the masters of a practical art for the benefit of actual sick persons.'[50] His criticism is perhaps well illustrated with the transformation of the 19th-century apothecary into today's general medical practitioner.

50 Ivan Illich, *Limits to Medicine. Medical Nemesis: the expropriation of health* (London: Marion Boyars Publishing, [1995] 2002) 253.

Chapter 6

The impact of the common law on the practice of medicine

'Who shall decide when doctors disagree?'[1]

Alexander Pope (1688–1744)

WE HAVE ALREADY SEEN THAT REGULATION OF THE MEDICAL profession, in legal terms or otherwise, did not really commence in earnest until the Apothecaries Act of 1815. The Medical Act of 1858, which brought with it the formation of the General Medical Council (as noted earlier), was the next piece of legislature to have a major impact on how medicine could be practised. However, although the ideal, as Wacks says, is for law to be 'clear, certain and comprehensible',[2] statute law is often ambiguous and open to interpretation.[3] It therefore should not be surprising that the area of law which, in this author's considered opinion (the details of which will be discussed below), has had the greatest influence over the nuances

1 Alexander Pope, *Peri Bathous* (The Art of Sinking in Poetry), 1727. In: Pat Rogers, editor, *Alexander Pope, The Major Works* (Oxford: Oxford University Press, 2006) 195–238.

2 Raymond Wacks, *Law: a very short introduction* (Oxford: Oxford University Press, 2008) 34.

3 It is suggested that there are three rules of statutory interpretation: The Literal Rule, The Golden (or Purposive) Rule and The Mischief Rule. These are defined in the above reference on page 31.

of medical practice since 1900 is the Common Law: law that has been appositely called 'the common-sense of the community, crystallised and formulated by our forefathers'.[4] It is the law as developed by the courts and the judiciary through the interpretation of statute law,[5] the application of the doctrine of precedent,[6] and the expectations of Herbert's[7] 'reasonable man'.[8]

The value of the common law is especially pertinent when it comes to the consideration of controversial medical issues (discussed below). In such cases, it may well be argued that 'Parliament is an unwilling participant and the courts must respond'.[9] Stauch *et al.* lists no less than 519 such cases which have had an impact on how medicine is practised.[10] Tovey distils the list down to 230.[11] However, new cases (e.g. the successful appeal to the House of Lords in 2009 by a patient with multiple sclerosis, who sought legal recognition in respect to her right to assisted suicide)[12] are being added all the time and the medico-legal tableau is one which is constantly in animation.

However, there are times when even the law lords are concerned that their judgments should not be taken as a representation of settled law. For example, on the subject of withholding life-prolonging treatment in a patient in a persistent vegetative state: 'It is imperative that the moral, social and legal issues of the present case should be considered by Parliament.'[13] And: 'I believe that adversarial proceedings, even with the help of an amicus curiae,[14] are not the right vehicle

4 Geoffrey Rivlin, *Understanding the Law*, 4th ed. (Oxford: Oxford University Press, 2006) 25.
5 Anthony King, *The British Constitution* (Oxford: Oxford University Press, 2007) 45.
6 Ian Mcleod, *Legal Method*, 6th ed. (Basingstoke: Macmillan, [1993] 2005) 129.
7 Arthur P Herbert, *Uncommon Law* (Kelly Bray: House of Stratus, [1935] 2001).
8 *See* note 4.
9 Ian Kennedy and Andrew Grubb, *Medical Law*, 3rd ed. (London: Butterworths, 2000) 6.
10 Marc Stauch, Kay Wheat and John Tingle, *Text, Cases and Materials on Medical Law*, 3rd ed. (Oxford: Routledge Cavendish, 2006) xix–xxx.
11 Gwyn Tovey, *Medical Law*, 1st ed. (London: Sweet & Maxwell, 2008) vii–xiv.
12 *R (on the application of Purdy) v DPP* [2009] UKHL 45.
13 *Per* Lord Browne-Wilkinson and Lord Mustill in *Airedale NHS Trust Respondents v Bland Appellant* [1993] 2 WLR 316.
14 *Amicus curiae:* 'Friend of the court. A non-party who gives evidence before the court so

for the discussion of this broad and highly contentious moral issue.'[15] The English jurisdiction is not alone in having such reservations. For example, in a similar issue in the United States Supreme Court, Scalia J said: 'These are problems properly decided by the citizens, through their elected representatives, not by the courts.'[16] Doctors must be alert to these legal uncertainties and be prepared to alter their medical practice in accordance with the latest legal decisions emanating from the courts.

That said, how then does the common law sit in relation to the practice of medicine? Is the common law helpful to the practice of medicine, fortifying the autonomy of the physicians, or does it serve to tighten the legal shackles referred to within the introductory paragraphs? To paraphrase the underlying question of this book: is the common law medicine's friend or nemesis? The answer to this comes from many different cases; the earliest of importance arguably was that of *Rose*,[17] which was discussed in an earlier chapter. It is not intended that more is said about it here apart from emphasising the major role it played in legally supporting the development of general medical practice.

There is clear evidence that some cases do nothing to detract from doctors' professional autonomy. Two cases involving consideration of capacity, *Re MB*[18] and *Re T*,[19] are good cases to illustrate this point.

In *Re MB* a pregnant woman was found to be incompetent and therefore unable to judge whether refusing to agree to a Caesarean section in order to deliver her child was an appropriate action. The *ratio decidendi* of the case was such that, whilst the court upheld the

as to assist it with research, argument or submissions.' *Oxford Dictionary of Law*, 6th ed. (2006).

15 *Per* Lord Mustill in *Airedale NHS Trust Respondents v Bland Appellant* [1993] 2 WLR 316 (at 890).

16 *Per* Scalia J in *Cruzan v Director, Missouri Department of Health* (1990) 110 S. Ct. 2841, 2859.

17 *William Rose v The College of Physicians*, London [1703] 2 ER 857.

18 *Re MB (A Patient)* [2005] EWCA Civ 1293.

19 *Re T (Adult: Refusal of Medical Treatment)* [1992] 4 All ER 649.

right of the pregnant woman to have the preservation of her own autonomy placed above any consideration of the well-being of the foetus, the court also upheld the right of the medical profession to make the decision over whether or not the woman had the capacity to actually make a reasoned decision and ultimately, by extrapolation, left the doctors with the power to decide on what course of action constituted the patient's best interest.[20]

In *Re T* the Court of Appeal's decision was again to uphold the 'absolute right'[21] of the patient (not suffering from mental illness) to decide whether to accept or reject any form of treatment. However, from this case, the court published a set of procedural guidelines for future reference, guidelines that indicated that the court was 'clearly disinclined to interfere in clinical matters'.[22]

Some judges have been seen as particularly supportive and protective of the medical profession. For example, Lord Donaldson[23] heard the appeals for both *Re R* and *Re W*.[24] In *Re W* the court authorised treatment of an anorexic girl against her wishes. In the course of his judgment, Lord Donaldson highlighted his support of the process of consent to treatment as giving doctors 'a legal flak jacket',[25] thereby placing him alongside Lord Denning[26] as judges who were 'concerned to protect the medical profession from the fire of litigation'.[27]

Lord Denning for his part clearly showed a depth of understanding and concern regarding the interrelationship between law and the medical profession[28] when he wrote in respect to the situation in the USA:

20 JK Mason and GT Laurie, *Law and Medical Ethics*, 7th ed. (Oxford: Oxford University Press, 2006) 380.
21 Ibid.: 373.
22 Ibid.: 382.
23 John Francis Donaldson, Baron Donaldson of Lymington, PC (1920–2005); Master of the Rolls 1982–92.
24 *Re W (A minor: Medical Treatment)* [1992] 4 All ER 627.
25 *Per* Donaldson in *Re W* (at 78).
26 Alfred Thompson Denning, Baron Denning OM, PC, DL (1899–1999); Master of the Rolls 1962–82.
27 *See* note 20: 371.
28 Otakar Hájek, Lord Denning and Medical Law, *Common Law Rev*, 2004; 5: 6.

> Medical malpractice suits there have become the curse of the medical profession. The legal profession get contingency fees. So they take up cases on speculation. The jury gives enormous damages. Insurance premiums are high. The doctors charge fees to cover them. It is all very worrying.[29]

Such concern was further illustrated in *Roe v Minister of Health,*[30] where, in his judgment, Lord Denning said: 'We should be doing a disservice to the community at large if we were to impose liability on hospitals and doctors for everything that happens to go wrong . . . we must not condemn as negligent that which is only misadventure.'[31] *Hatcher v Black,*[32] a case involving an allegation of negligence, was another occasion where Denning LJ strongly supported the medical profession, stating that the law only condemns a doctor 'when he falls short of the accepted standards of a great profession', and not 'when he only does that which many a wise and good doctor so placed would do'.[33]

Statements such as those in *Hatcher* and *Roe* were cited in the landmark case of *Bolam,*[34] which firmly established (at least until developed by *Bolitho*[35] in 1997) the legal position in respect to negligence by doctors. Based on a fundamental principle within the tort of negligence[36] dating back to 1909 in another jurisdiction,[37] the 'Bolam Test'[38] was a strongly supportive one in respect to recognising the autonomy of the medical profession, with McNair J phrasing the principle as: 'a doctor is not guilty of negligence if he has acted in accordance with a practice accepted as proper by a responsible body

29 Lord Denning, *The Discipline of Law* (Oxford: Oxford University Press, 1979).
30 *Roe v Minister of Health* [1954] 2 QB 66.
31 *Per* Denning, op. cit.: 87.
32 *Hatcher v Black* [1954] Queen's Bench Division; reported in *The Times*, 2 July 1954.
33 *Per* Denning, ibid.
34 *Bolam v Friern Hospital Management Committee* [1957] 1 WLR 582.
35 *Bolitho v City and Hackney Health Authority* [1997] 4 All ER 771 9HL.
36 Michael A Jones, *Medical Negligence*, 4th ed. (London: Sweet & Maxwell, 2008) 230.
37 *Morton v William Dixon Ltd* 1909 SC 807.
38 Michael Davies, *Medical Law*, 2nd ed. (Oxford: Oxford University Press, 1998) 86.

of medical men skilled in that particular art.' Lord Denning echoed the sentiment of *Bolam* in his speech in *Whitehouse v Jordan*,[39] when he said: 'I would suggest that you ask the average competent and careful practitioner: "Is this the sort of mistake that you yourself might have made?" If he says "Yes, even doing the best I could, it might have happened to me", then he is not negligent.'[40] However, *Bolitho* ushered in a subtle change in the way the courts approached the Bolam Test, signalling a change in the relationship between the medical profession and the courts.[41] No longer were the courts willing to simply accept an action as being acceptable to a 'responsible body of medical men'. Instead, the courts reserved the right to determine whether the view taken by that 'responsible body' was a logical and defensible one: 'if it can be demonstrated that the professional opinion is not capable of withstanding logical analysis, the judge is entitled to hold that the body of opinion is not reasonable or responsible'.[42]

In 1997, the courts were therefore stating quite clearly that the issue of 'reasonableness' is a matter for the court and not for the medical profession. It is possibly fair to suggest that the latter is just one small part of the drive within common law to reduce the autonomous status of the medical profession and to render it more answerable to the courts. A decade previously, Donaldson MR had made clear his view on the issue of the definition of 'duty of care', stating that it was a definition determined by the law and not by the doctors. In his view, the law: 'could not stand by if the profession, by an excess of paternalism, denied their patients a real choice'.[43] The drive by the courts to ensure that patients are offered a 'real choice' by doctors took a further turn in 2004, when the concept of 'informed consent' was considered by the House of Lords in respect to a case of

39 *Whitehouse v Jordan* [1980] 1 All ER 650.
40 *Per* Lord Denning in *Whitehouse v Jordan* at 658.
41 *See* note 12: 73.
42 *Per* Lord Browne-Wilkinson in *Bolitho* at 243.
43 *Per* Donaldson MR in *Sidaway v Board of Governors of the Bethlem Royal Hospital and the Maudsley Hospital and Others* [1984] QB 493 at 513.

causation and negligence. For some authors, *Chester v Afshar*[44] was a watershed and threatened a sea change in the standard applicable to information disclosure in English law.[45]

The process of obtaining consent to a procedure has long been considered a necessity in order for doctors to avoid the tort of battery.[46] Although the latter is a matter of debate,[47] a debate compounded by the transatlantic notion of 'informed consent',[48] the 'but for' test[49] had heretofore prevented a causal link between any failure in the process of obtaining consent and a successful accusation of negligence in respect to injury occurring from known risks associated with a given procedure;[50] it had been taken by the courts that the first fault did not directly lead to the second.

However, in *Chester v Afshar* a neurosurgeon was accused by a patient of failing to fully inform her of all the risks (however small) associated with a proposed surgical procedure, and that, as a result, she had experienced injury that she would have otherwise avoided. Despite the fact that the risk was one which could happen without any suggestion of negligence during the performance of the procedure, the patient claimed that, had she been fully informed of all the risks, she would have chosen not to undergo the proposed operation. The judges decided in the plaintiff's favour by a majority of one.

Whilst the Bristol Royal Infirmary Inquiry[51] had previously brought the concept of informed consent into focus within England,

44 *Chester v Afshar* [2004] 4 All ER 58 HL.

45 Robert M Jaggs-Fowler, *A Critical Evaluation of the Majority Decision in Chester v Afshar: a sea-change for information disclosure standards in English Law?* (Unpublished, LLM Assignment, De Montfort University, 2010).

46 JK Mason and GT Laurie, *Law and Medical Ethics*, 7th ed. (Oxford: Oxford University Press, 2006) 393.

47 Michael A Jones, *Medical Negligence*, 4th ed. (London: Sweet & Maxwell, 2008) 558.

48 *See* note 12: 68–74.

49 The 'but for' test: would the plaintiff have suffered the injury but for the negligent action of the accused?

50 Emily Jackson, *Medical Law* (Oxford: Oxford University Press, 2006) 141–7.

51 Bristol Royal Infirmary Inquiry, *Learning from Bristol: the report of the public inquiry into children's heart surgery of the Bristol Royal Infirmary, 1984–1995* (London: HMSO, 2001).

the subject had remained one of academic and political debate.[52] *Chester v Afshar* brought the debate into the arena of the courts, with Lords Steyn, Hope and Walker forming the opinion that, in keeping with the principle of respect for autonomy,[53] it was the duty of the doctor to warn of all the risks. Failing to do so deprived the patient of her Millian Liberalist[54] right to self-determination,[55] (that is, should damage subsequently occur, the patient would be entitled to compensation (damages) on the grounds that the 'but for' test had been satisfied). The dissenting voices of Lords Bingham[56] and Hoffman provided some small comfort for doctors:

> The purpose of a duty to warn someone against the risk involved in what he proposes to do . . . is to give him an opportunity to avoid that risk. If he would have been unable or unwilling to take that opportunity and the risk eventuates, the failure to warn has not caused the damage. It would have happened anyway.[57]

Nevertheless, in the main, the legal pendulum was swinging away from the established professionally based Bolam[58] standard, and with it, what might be termed the 'special relationship' that the medical profession enjoyed with the courts through the likes of Lord Denning and Lord Donaldson. If any doubt of the latter exists,

52 In a debate in the House of Commons on 18 July 2001, the Health Secretary of the day, Alan Milburn MP, said 'informed consent must be a cornerstone of a modern health service' (Hansard, Vol. 372, cols. 289–304, available at: http://hansard.millbanksystems.com/commons/2001/jul/18/bristol-royal-informary-inquiry, accessed: 25 September 2010).

53 Tom L Beauchamp and James F Childress, *Principles of Biomedical Ethics*, 6th ed. (Oxford: Oxford University Press, 2009) 74.

54 De Montfort University, LLM Handbook, *Introduction to Health Care Law and Ethics* (Leicester: De Montfort University, 2008) 33.

55 Dan W Brock, 'An ethical framework for treatment decision-making', In: Helga Kuhse and Peter Singer, editors, *A Companion to Bioethics* (Oxford: Blackwell, [1998] 2001) 232.

56 *Per* Lord Bingham in *Chester v Afshar* [2004] UKHL 41 at paragraph 8: *'It is now . . . generally accepted that the "but for" test does not provide a comprehensive or exclusive test of causation in the law of tort'.*

57 *Per* Lord Hoffman in *Chester v Afshar* [2004] UKHL 41 at paragraph 28.

58 Kenyon Mason and Douglas Brodie, *Bolam, Bolam* – Wherefore Art Thou *Bolam*? *Edin L Rev*, 2005; 9: 398.

one only needs to compare the tone of the statement made by Lord Donaldson in *Sidaway*: '[the law] could not stand by if the profession, by an excess of paternalism, denied their patients a real choice'[59] with the far more dogmatic (albeit *obiter* comment) made by Lord Steyn in *Chester*: 'the court is the final arbiter of what constitutes informed consent'.[60] From the medical profession's viewpoint, with *Chester*, the common law had just escalated the perceived legal threat in respect to issues surrounding the topic of informed consent, even though there was (and is) no legal definition of the latter in English law.[61] As Mason and Brodie put it, '*Bolam* has left the medical jurisprudential arena.'[62]

That said, there is the faint suggestion that the aforementioned death notice for *Bolam* may have been premature, for, one year after *Chester*, the judgment in *Gregg v Scott*[63] offered the medical profession a glimmer of salvation. Whilst in *Gregg* the Lords considered *Chester*, it was deemed that *Chester* was: 'dealing with a particular problem which could be remedied without altering the principles applicable to the great majority of personal injury cases which give rise to no real injustice or practical problem.'[64] Furthermore, the Lords maintained that: 'a claim for damages for clinical negligence required proof on a balance of probability that the negligence was the cause of the adverse consequences complained of . . .'.[65] *Chester* and *Gregg* therefore appear to have incompatible judgments. If this is the case, it raises the possibility that *Chester* was wrongly decided.[66] Be that so it may, on the subject of informed consent, the medical profession has heeded the barking of a less-than-friendly court. The General Medical Council

59 *Per* Donaldson MR in *Sidaway v Board of Governors of the Bethlem Royal Hospital* [1984] QB 493 at 513.
60 *Per* Lord Steyn in *Chester v Afshar* [2004] 4 All ER 58 HL at paragraph 14.
61 *See* note 11: 74.
62 *See* note 58: 302.
63 *Gregg v Scott* [2005] UKHL 2.
64 *Per* Baroness Hale in *Gregg v Scott* at paragraph 192.
65 *See* note 12: 139–40.
66 Ibid.: 140.

has seen fit to issue updated guidance[67] on the issue of consent, recognising that 'the highest duty applies to warning patients of all known risks',[68] and even the NHS Litigation Authority issued a 'Risk Alert' to doctors.[69]

Ironically, all of the above could turn out to be in the medical profession's favour. In 1985, Teff described what he saw as a need for a 'therapeutic alliance' between doctors and their patients.[70] His concept found favour with other academics who saw a need to end the 'spirit of confrontation'[71] between the two parties. To this aim, the law could well turn out to be medicine's friend. In 1999, a search of the Medical Law Reports for the 14-year period after *Sidaway* revealed 30 cases of alleged negligence whereby the topic of 'informed consent' was invoked.[72] A similar search by the author of the years January 2000 to September 2010 found a further 34 cases within the English jurisdiction (16 of which occurred after *Chester*), 2 in the Scottish courts and 1 in the European Court of Human Rights.[73] As has been written elsewhere,[74] a rudimentary analysis of these figures shows an incidence for such cases of 2.1 cases per year in the 14 years after *Sidaway*, compared to 3.4 cases per year in my 10-year search period, but representing only 2.7 cases per year in the English courts during the 6 years following *Chester*. The simplistic quality of the statistical analysis is open to criticism; however, it does not detract from the fact

67 General Medical Council, *Consent: patients and doctors making decisions together* (London: GMC, 2008).

68 Rosamund Rhodes-Kemp, Why consent matters, *Law Society Gazette*, 6 April 2006 [online] (Available at: www.lawgazette.co.uk/opinion/comment/why-consent-matters, accessed: 4 August 2010).

69 NHS Litigation Authority, *NHSLA Risk Alert: informed consent* (London: NHS Litigation Authority, 2004).

70 H Teff, Consent in medical procedures: paternalism, self-determination or therapeutic alliance? *Law Q Rev*, 1985; 101: 432.

71 JK Mason and GT Laurie, *Law and Medical Ethics*, 7th ed. (Oxford: Oxford University Press, 2006) 411.

72 Michael Jones, Informed consent and other fairy tales, *Med Law Rev*, 1999; 7: 121–2.

73 These cases are listed under a separate heading within the Bibliography.

74 Robert M Jaggs-Fowler, *A Critical Evaluation of the Majority Decision in Chester v Afshar: a sea-change for information disclosure standards in English Law?* (Unpublished, LLM Assignment, De Montfort University, 2010).

that the law has a 'symbolic significance',[75] and that doctors will take notice and adjust their behaviour if it is perceived that they would otherwise be open to litigation. At least in this way, the common law can be deemed to serve as medicine's beneficent guide.

There are, of course, other areas of medical practice wherein the common law has influenced the behaviour of doctors. Whilst it is not the intention to provide a comprehensive study of all such facets, it would be remiss not to refer to one or two major issues which assist in reflecting the complex relationship between the law and medicine.

Up until 1986, the provision of contraceptive services to minors under the age of 16 years was fraught with difficulties from a medico-legal perspective, not only because of the legal age of consent to sexual intercourse,[76] but also in view of the fact that statute law[77] only gave minors over the age of 16 years the right to consent to treatment without recourse to a parental opinion. For those minors aged 13–16 years,[78] there is no statutory law relating to their ability to consent to contraceptive treatment without parental consent.[79] For a long time, therefore, many doctors were acting out of a sense of beneficence by providing contraceptive treatment to minors under 16 years without their parental consent, whilst at the same time running the (at least theoretical) risk of legal action against them.[80] The case of *Gillick v*

---

75 *See* note 72: 130.

76 The general legal age of consent to sexual activity is 16 years. Richard Card, *Criminal Law*, 18th ed. (Oxford: Oxford University Press, 2008) 337. However, up until 1956, the laws relating to sexual offences were contained within several different statutes, including the Age of Marriage Act 1929 and the Children and Young Persons Act 1933. These (and others) were consolidated in the Sexual Offences Act 1956, which in turn was largely repealed by the Sexual Offences Act 2003.

77 Family Law Reform Act 1969, s. 8(1).

78 Sexual intercourse with a child under the age of 13 years is statutory rape under the Sexual Offences Act 2003, s. 5. David Ormerod, *Smith & Hogan Criminal Law*, 12th ed. (Oxford: Oxford University Press, 2008) 708.

79 Lorraine Corfield, Ingrid Granne and William Latimer-Sayer, *ABC of Medical Law* (Oxford: Blackwell, 2009) 2.

80 The concern was that the doctor would be committing an offence under s. 28(1) of the Sexual Offences Act 1956, or of aiding and abetting unlawful sexual intercourse contrary to s. 6 of the same Act, or under s. 8 of the Family Law Reform Act 1969 (The Law Society, Social Security Law – some legal principles in *Gillick*: A Guide – Part 1, *Law Society Gazette*, 1987, 29 Apr (84): 1245).

West Norfolk and Wisbech Area Health Authority[81] provided the law which prevails today and, in so doing, offered doctors a medico-legal yardstick (through the concept of Gillick Competence,[82] also known as the Fraser Rules[83]) by which they could practise with a reduced risk of litigation.[84]

The subject of consent has raised issues in other ways apart from the topics of informed consent and consent to contraceptive treatment by minors under 16 years.

In 2003, the courts supported doctors trying to act in the best interests of a child, despite only having the consent of one parent. The case, *B (a child)*,[85] involved the immunisation of a child against the wishes of one parent. The judge supported the proposed action of the doctors, whilst indicating that future cases of a similar nature should still be brought before a court. This would ensure that, whilst recognising and supporting the doctors in their endeavours, the courts would have an opportunity to ensure that all material issues were considered, thereby ensuring justice for the families as well.

Two cases in other jurisdictions, which have contained salutary lessons for doctors working under the English jurisdiction, are *Mohr v Williams*[86] and *Brushett v Cowan*,[87] both of which relate to the timing and purpose of the consent given. In the former, consent was obtained for an operation on the patient's right ear. However, the

81 *Gillick v West Norfolk and Wisbech Area Health Authority* [1986] 1 AC 112.

82 Shaun D Pattinson, *Medical Law and Ethics* (London: Sweet & Maxwell, 2006) 160.

83 *Per* Lord Fraser in *Gillick* at 844: a health professional can provide contraceptive advice and treatment to a person under the age of 16 who refused to inform her parents, as long as: '(1) that the girl (although under 16 years of age) will understand his advice; (2) that he cannot persuade her to inform her parents or to allow him to inform the parents that she is seeking contraceptive advice; (3) that she is very likely to begin or to continue having sexual intercourse with or without contraceptive treatment; (4) that unless she receives contraceptive advice or treatment her physical or mental health or both are likely to suffer; (5) that her best interest require him to give her contraceptive advice, treatment or both without the parental consent'.

84 Jo Bridgeman, Young people and sexual health: whose rights? Whose responsibilities? *Med Law Rev* 2006, 14(3): 418–24.

85 *B (a child) (Welfare of child: Immunisation)* [2003] EWCA Civ 1148.

86 *Mohr v Williams* [1905] 104 NW 12 (Supp. Ct. Minn.).

87 *Brushett v Cowan* [1991] 2 Med LR 271 (Newfoundland, CA).

surgeon additionally operated on a lesion on the left ear, an action for which he was successfully sued for battery as the second operation went beyond the purpose of the original consent. In the second case, consent was obtained for a muscle biopsy; however, the surgeon also biopsied an abnormal area of bone. In this case, a charge of battery was not sustained as the purpose of the original consent was to ascertain what was wrong with the patient.

In both cases, it might be claimed that the surgeon was acting in accordance with the principle of beneficence. However, the courts' decisions indicate that beneficence alone is not a protection from litigation – a patient's right of autonomy is equally, if not more, important. Where that right is not upheld by the medical profession, the courts are likely to find in favour of the plaintiff. Conversely, where the doctor has acted in accordance with the patient's principal desire (e.g. in *Brushett*, the desire to have a diagnosis made), then the courts are likely to support the doctor: the principle of justice, it might be said, being seen to be upheld.

Other areas of medical practice have presented doctors with difficult dilemmas with which the courts have been able to lend assistance in the finding of a solution. One such area is the provision of specific medical treatment at the patient's request when doctors consider such treatment to be futile. In *Burke v GMC*,[88] the *ratio decidendi* was that, whilst a doctor who deliberately stops life-sustaining treatment against the clear wishes of a competent patient would face a charge of murder, a patient cannot demand specific medical treatment at any time. That said, the courts also reserve the right to determine whether life-sustaining treatment can be lawfully withdrawn in cases where the patient has lost capacity. Where agreed to by the courts, a doctor can stop such treatment without fear of a charge of murder or manslaughter. *Airedale NHS Trust v Bland*[89] is one such example

88 *Burke v GMC* [2005] EWCA Civ 1003.
89 *Airedale NHS Trust v Bland* [1993] AC 789.

where the assistance of the courts has been invaluable to the medical profession.

CONCLUSION

Whilst the above discussion has been by no means all-inclusive, the cases presented do serve to indicate that, through the common law, the law can be of immense assistance to the medical profession when it comes to the clarification of the appropriate way forward in respect to medical issues wherein there are difficult moral and/or ethical dilemmas. By following lines of action which have previously been accepted as legal precedents, or by seeking a specific judgment from the courts in cases of doubt, doctors can be reasonably sure that their actions are going to be supported in law. In this respect, the law has shown, by the clear setting of medico-legal boundaries, that it can most certainly be regarded as the medical profession's trusted guide. By practising within the precincts of those boundaries, the law allows doctors the freedom to make decisions and take action as they feel best fits the interests of their patients.

By the same token, the law has also clearly shown that it is prepared to take a condemnatory view of doctors who act outside of the law, or who risk acting at times of ethical uncertainty without first seeking a legal opinion.

From a common law perspective, the law may, on balance, be considered as the medical profession's friend. However, the law's friendship in this respect is not without reservation, and it clearly reserves the right of admonition.

Ultimately, in respect to Alexander Pope's question as to 'who shall decide when doctors disagree?' (noted earlier), it is suggested that the resounding and unequivocal answer is 'the common law'.

Chapter 7

The impact of statute law on the practice of medicine

'Freedom is about authority. Freedom is about the willingness of every single human being to cede to lawful authority a great deal of discretion about what you do and how you do it.'[1]

Rudy Giuliani, Mayor of New York (1994–2001)

AS OF 2005, THERE WERE 48 STATUTES,[2] 20 STATUTORY INSTRUMENTS,[3] and numerous Department of Health circulars and guidelines, General Medical Council codes of practice and other guidance, and international declarations, conventions and protocols[4] directly regulating various aspects of medical practice within the 21st century. More, including the NHS Act 2006, the Mental Health Act 2007, Human Fertilisation and Embryology Act 2008, and Health and Social Care Act 2008, have since been added, and the count contin-

1 Rudy Giuliani, speech at a forum on crime in the cities, quoted in: *The New York Times*, 20 March 1994 (www.nytimes.com/1994/03/20/nyregion/freedom-is-about-authority-excerpts-from-giuliani-speech-on-crime.html).

2 Michael A Jones and Anne E Morris, *Blackstone's Statutes on Medical Law*, 4th ed. (Oxford: Oxford University Press, 2005) v.

3 Ibid.: vi.

4 Ibid.: vi–vii.

ues.[5] These figures include the laws concerning homicide, driving offences, sexual offences, theft, fraud, criminal damage, corporate liability and complicity.[6]

If Giuliani's statement about freedom (the epigraph) is correct, the immediate conclusion must be that, by virtue of the statistics in the opening paragraph of this chapter, doctors have never before experienced such an extent of freedom. In philosophical terms, that may well be true. However, it also presents a paradox. For, as each year brings new legislation, the chains which upset Rousseau's equilibrium in 1762[7] are added to link by legislated link. Perhaps the answer lies in knowledge or, more precisely, the acquisition of medico-legal knowledge by medical practitioners. It may be argued that the greater an individual's knowledge of a subject, the greater is their understanding of where the boundaries are positioned; being more informed brings greater confidence, and thus the more relaxed doctors can be in the practice of medicine within those boundaries. The freedom is not for doctors to do as they will, but to know that what they do within the legislated boundaries is acceptable to society and the laws of society; for the law-abiding doctor, true freedom in this sense may thus be considered psychological, not physical, in its manifestation.[8]

The problem, however, is how do we know what we do not know?[9] Or, to be more precise, how do doctors know that they are fully aware

5 Anne E Morris and Michael A Jones, *Blackstone's Statutes on Medical Law*, 6th ed. (Oxford: Oxford University Press, 2009) v.

6 Ibid. *See* pages vii–ix for a list of the current statutes, statutory instruments, Department of Health Circulars and Guidelines, General Medical Council Codes and Guidance, Codes of Practice, and International Protocols. Additional material is available online at: www.oup.com/uk/orc/bin/statutes/books/10medical/additional (accessed: 10 October 2010).

7 See the opening quotation in Chapter 2.

8 However, such issues start to impinge on the metaphysical topics of freedom and determinism, and in-depth philosophical discussions of this nature are not truly appropriate to the subject of this book. I have therefore taken the liberty of keeping such statements as superficial. Further analytical discourse can be found in: Roy Weatherford, *The Implications of Determinism* (London: Routledge, 1991), and in Mortimer J Adler, *The Idea of Freedom* (New York: Doubleday, 1958).

9 JER Squires, Understanding, in Ted Honderich, editor, *The Oxford Companion to Philosophy* (Oxford: Oxford University Press, 1995) 886.

of all the legal issues impacting on their practice of medicine? After all, as Selden[10] wrote, 'ignorance of the law excuses no man'.[11] It is recognised that keeping up to date with developments in medical law (in addition to the myriad of changes within the discipline of medicine) is 'no easy task'[12] and 'virtually impossible for even the most conscientious of doctors',[13] and that training for doctors in respect to new legislation is scarce.[14]

Yet, that very task has not necessarily become any harder over the past 180 years since the publication of Willcock's *Laws Relating to the Medical Profession*.[15] In 1870, Weightman recognised that the passage of just 40 years had rendered Willcock's book obsolete.[16] In his own publication, Weightman listed 51 statutes[17] (in addition to the 197 listed cases)[18] that he considered pertinent to the practice of medicine in the late 19th century. However, which doctor in the 21st century would now instantly recognise his legal obligations under the Lunacy Acts,[19] the Sanitary Acts,[20] the Copyright Acts,[21] the Contagious Diseases Acts,[22] the Vaccinations Acts,[23] the Poor

---

10 John Selden (1584–1654), English jurist and philosopher.

11 John Selden, 'Tabletalk', p. 2041. In: David Wilkins, editor, *Opera Omnia Seldeni* (*The Works of John Selden Esq. in Three Volumes*), Vol. 3 (Clark, NJ: Lawbook Exchange, 2006) Part 3.

12 Vivienne Harpwood, *Medicine, Malpractice and Misapprehensions* (Oxford: Routledge-Cavendish, 2007) 134.

13 Ibid.: 162.

14 Vivienne Harpwood, 'In Defence of Doctors'. In: Sheila AM McLean, editor, *First Do No Harm: law, ethics and healthcare* (Aldershot: Ashgate, 2006) 587.

15 JW Willcock, *The Laws Relating to the Medical Profession* (London: Clarke, 1830).

16 Hugh Weightman, *The Medical Practitioners' Legal Guide* (London: Renshaw, 1870) iii.

17 Ibid.: xvii–xviii.

18 Ibid.: xv–xvi.

19 The Lunacy Act 1845 (8 & 9 Vict. c. 100) and the County Asylums Act 1845 constituted the mental health law in England from 1845 to 1890.

20 The Sanitary Act 1866 (29 & 30 Vict. c. 90) and the Sanitary Act 1868 (31 & 32 Vict. c. 115), related to the setting up of Health Boards by local authorities.

21 The Copyright Act 1842 (5 & 6 Vict. c. 45), also known as Talfourd's Act, protected the copyright for the authors of medical writing. The International Copyright Act 1852 (15 & 16 Vict. c. 12) introduced the concept of translation rights.

22 The Contagious Diseases Act 1866 (29 & 30 Vict. c. 35) allowed for the detention of persons suffering from venereal disease, amended the Contagious Diseases Act 1864, and had alterations made to it by a 1969 Act.

23 The Vaccination Acts were 3 & 4 Vict. c. 29; 4 & 5 Vict. c. 32 and 16 & 17 Vict. c. 100. All

Law Acts[24] or the Will Act?[25] All of these Weightman listed as being newly topical for the practising doctor in 1870.[26] (Ironically, of them all, it is probably the Copyright Acts with which many doctors will be most familiar!)

Nonetheless, there is an argument in favour of the growing complexity of statutory regulation. The latter is necessitated by the similarly growing convolutions of society, along with the intricacies that scientific developments can offer society. The society of the early 21st century is one containing numerous facets that a 16th-century doctor would hardly recognise. Freedom for the physicians first made its appearance with the passage of the laws of Henry VIII (*see* Chapter 4), and then for the early general practitioners in the early 19th century with the Apothecaries Act of 1815. Such laws protected their right to practise, and hence gave them a professional existence free from the concern of litigation simply on the grounds of their practising medicine. For today's doctors, the freedom sought is not so much as the right to practise per se, but the right to practise utilising certain modern scientific advances (such as genetic engineering), or the right to cater for changes in society's collective philosophical and moralistic standing (e.g. in respect to assisted suicide). Whilst the common law can accommodate and reflect some of the simpler changes required by a metamorphic society, it is evident that the learned deliberations of three or five judges is insufficient when it comes to the more momentous decisions which have to be made in order to reflect that societal transformation. As Lord Mustill stated in *Airedale NHS Trust v Bland* (*see* Chapter 5), there are certain matters which:

of these were consolidated into the Vaccination Act 1867 (30 & 31 Vict. c. 84). They all related to the compulsory vaccination of children for smallpox.

24 The Poor Law Amendment Act 1834 transformed England's system of poverty relief, central to which was the work-house, and considered the appointment of medical officers to the same. Various amendments and additions were made to the 1834 Act by the Poor Law Act 1835 and the Poor Law Amendment Act 1844.

25 The Will Act 1837 (1 Vict. c. 26).

26 Hugh Weightman, *The Medical Practitioners' Legal Guide* (London: Renshaw, 1870) iv.

> cry out for exploration in depth by Parliament and then for the establishment by legislation not only of a new set of ethically and intellectually consistent rules, distinct from the criminal law, but also of a sound procedural framework within which the rules can be applied to individual cases.[27]

It may well be that Lord Mustill's comments are most pertinent when it comes to matters such as end-of-life decisions. However, they are not always easily put into action. Even the legislature prefers not to confront certain ethical issues,[28] as witnessed by the difficulties experienced with the Medical Treatment (Prevention of Euthanasia) Bill[29] (the latter being found to be 'confused and unhelpful').[30] Nonetheless, the failure of such debate to bring about new legislation does not necessarily imply unfettered freedom for the medical profession when it comes to such matters. What it does mean is that, if doctors are going to act within the law, each new case must be given consideration within a court of law; actions arising from a doctor's own volition could easily see that doctor falling foul of the criminal law under such statutes as the Homicide Act 1957, as Dr John Bodkin Adams,[31] Dr Leonard Arthur,[32] Dr Thomas Lodwig[33] and Dr Harold Shipman[34] discovered (albeit, for different motives).[35]

---

27 *Per* Lord Mustill at 889 in: *Airedale Trust v Bland* [1993] 1 All ER 821.

28 Anne Morris, Easing the Passing: end of life decisions and the Medical Treatment (Prevention of Euthanasia) Bill, *Med Law Rev*, 2000; 8: 301.

29 The Medical Treatment (Prevention of Euthanasia) Bill was a Private Member's Bill introduced to Parliament in 1999 by Ann Winterton MP and attracted much opposition by many organisations including the BMA.

30 *See* note 28: 314.

31 *R v Adams* [1957] Crim LR 365. An interesting reflection of the trial by the trial judge can be found in: Patrick Devlin, *Easing the Passing: the trial of Dr John Bodkin Adams* (London: Bodley Head, 1985).

32 *R v Arthur* (1981) The Times, 5 November 1981.

33 *R v Lodwig* (1990) The Times, 16 March 1990.

34 *R v Dr Harold Shipman* (1999) – *The Shipman Enquiry* (London: Department of Health, 2002) (Available at: www.the-shipman-inquiry.org.uk/home.asp, accessed: 16 October 2010).

35 (i) 160 of Dr John Bodkin Adams patients died in suspicious circumstances; 132 of them left him money or items of value in their will. He was tried and acquitted on one count of murder in 1957. (ii) Dr Leonard Arthur was tried and acquitted for the attempted

…ains the case, however, that statute law (i.e. law made by Acts …ment), remains the primary legislation, legally trumping all …nt case law before it. It might be argued, however, that part of the preparatory work leading to some statute law is the debate that has waged within various common law cases, thereby dissecting the various facets of a particular subject until it is far clearer as to what constitutes an acceptable line for the government of the day to take. The strength of argument doctors can bring to common law cases can therefore be influential in structuring future statute law, and therein lays the power in shaping how medico-legal freedom should appear. The Mental Capacity Act 2005 is a good example, being shaped by countless common law cases in respect to issues of competence and capacity to consent.[36]

The Abortion Act 1967 is another good example of where a statute works in the favour of the medical profession and legitimises doctors' freedom to act in the best interest of their patients by providing a defence in law. The Act is structured in such a way as to specify the circumstances under which abortion is lawful, but at the same time having those criteria couched in such open phraseology as to give great flexibility of interpretation to the attending doctor[37] (initially, where the pregnancy had not reached 28 weeks, although this was reduced to 24 weeks in 1990).[38]

Another statute of potential benefit to the medical profession,

---

murder of a newborn child with Down syndrome. (iii) Dr Thomas Lodwig was accused of murdering a cancer patient, but acquitted for the absence of evidence at the trial. (iv) Dr Harold Shipman was found guilty of 15 murders, with another 203 being ascribed to him; in one case he was found to have altered a patient's will.

36 For example, *Airedale Trust v Bland* [1993] AC 789 HL, *B v An NHS Trust* (2002) 152 NLJ 470, *Gillick v West Norfolk and Wisbech AHA* [1986] 1 AC 112 HL, *Re T (adult: refusal of medical Treatment)* [1992] 4 All ER 64, *Re F (Mental Patient: Sterilisation)* [1990] 2 AC 1.

37 The Act provided a defence for doctors where abortion is necessary:
- to save the woman's life
- to prevent grave permanent injury to the woman's physical or mental health
- under 28 weeks to avoid injury to the physical or mental health of the woman
- under 28 weeks to avoid injury to the physical or mental health of the existing child(ren)
- if the child was likely to be severely physically or mentally handicapped.

38 The Human Fertilisation and Embryology Act 1990 amended the 1967 Abortion Act.

albeit more directly designed to control the problems caused by the increasing 'compensation culture'[39] in England, is the Compensation Act 2006. The Act introduced a statutory approach to the way judges apply the concept of 'standard of care' in medical negligence cases. It has been suggested that the Act essentially places into primary legislation the standards laid down in *Bolam*,[40] which, of course, is of advantage to the medical profession in view of the increasing attacks perceived to be taking place against the Bolam principle (as discussed in Chapter 5).

Conversely, it is also true that some statute law exists because of the very fact that certain established medical activities have been found to be unacceptable by society. In such cases, doctors have, in a manner of speaking, scored own goals, thereby having certain freedoms deliberately curtailed by Acts of Parliament as a result of having undertaking such action. The Human Tissue Act 2004 is a good example, arising directly from the Bristol Royal Infirmary Inquiry[41] and the Royal Liverpool Children's Inquiry[42] into the removal of organs from dead bodies, and the indefinite retention of such tissue. The circumstances behind both inquiries provoked substantial public outcry,[43] with the result that primary legislation was enacted to curtail doctors' activities, and hence their professional freedom. Although the retention of organs was, and still is, legal, doctors can now only undertake such activity with the consent of relatives of the deceased.

Occasionally, statute law invokes controversy as well as providing power for the medical profession, as with the Mental Health Act of

39 Editorial, Compensation culture: who's to blame? *BBC News* [online], 15 November 2000. Available at: http://news.bbc.co.uk/1/hi/uk/1024540.stm, accessed: 16 October 2010.

40 *See* note 14: 204.

41 Bristol Royal Infirmary Inquiry, *Learning from Bristol: the report of the public inquiry into children's heart surgery of the Bristol Royal Infirmary, 1984–1995* (London: HMSO, 2001).

42 *The Royal Liverpool Children's Inquiry Report* (London: Stationery Office, 2001) (www.rlcinquiry.org.uk, accessed: 22 June 2010).

43 Mary Riddell, Demonising doctors, *Guardian* [online], 4 February 2001, available at: www.guardian.co.uk/society/2001/feb/04/health.comment, accessed: 16 October 2010.

1983. In respect to the latter, Bartlett and Sandland have suggested that the Act 'masks the reality of medical freedom with the appearance of legal controls'.[44] Whilst it may be argued that the Act simply acknowledges and legitimises the 'authoritative power of medicine',[45] this does the profession no favours in the eyes of critics such as Szasz,[46] who has vehemently condemned the role of doctors in what he classed as the 'therapeutic state'.[47] Of course, such criticism is not confined to the current mental health laws (including the Mental Health 2007); the Lunacy Act 1890, Mental Deficiency Act 1913 and Mental Health Act 1959 were all statutes which (rightly or wrongly) empowered doctors to act on behalf of the state in respect to controlling undesirable personalities.[48]

Sometimes, however, the issues being considered by the legislature are not significant moral or ethical issues, but nonetheless of extreme significance to all medical practitioners. The subject of regulation of the medical profession is a topical case in point. For the past decade or so, much debate has taken place concerning the standard of medical self-regulation; which has culminated in the process of licensing,[49] re-licensing[50] and five-yearly revalidation.[51] The debate has often revolved around whether the revised process of regulation should be on a statutory footing.[52] Some commentators have taken the view that statutory regulation is a 'curate's egg':[53] 'Statutory self-

44 Peter Bartlett and Ralph Sandland, *Mental Health Law*, 3rd ed. (Oxford: Oxford University Press, 2007) 347.
45 Ibid.: 345.
46 Thomas Szasz (1920–), Hungarian-American psychiatrist, academic and social critic, and an early member of the anti-psychiatry movement.
47 Thomas Szasz, 'Curing the Therapeutic State', interview in *Reason Magazine*, 1963.
48 This controversial subject has been explored in greater detail by me in an LLM Assignment in 2009, details of which are given in the Bibliography.
49 General Medical Council, *Licensing* [online]. Available at: www.gmc-uk.org/doctors/licensing.asp, accessed: 26 October 2010.
50 Ibid..
51 General Medical Council, *Revalidation* [online]. Available at: www.gmc-uk.org/doctors/7330.asp, accessed: 26 October 2010.
52 David Price, Legal aspects of the regulation of the health professions. In: Judith Allsop and Mike Saks, editors, *Regulating the Health Professions* (London: Sage, 2002) 50.
53 Ibid.: 51.

regulation is a strong mechanism in protecting the public, but it is also heavy-handed and cumbersome . . . it is restrictive to individuals . . . provides a barrier to individuals' choice of work . . . it is costly . . .'[54] On the other hand, statutory self-regulation can also be empowering and therefore work in the profession's favour. Historically, several statutes have been of this nature, namely the Apothecaries Act 1815, the Pharmacy Act 1852, and the Medical Act 1858; all of these have brought benefits to the medical profession (as discussed in earlier chapters). As Price has commented: 'the statutory foundation of a regulatory scheme signals that a direct democratic mandate has been extended to the professional body concerned'.[55]

Finally, there are some statutes that simply overrule the medical profession's usual desire to protect patient confidentiality. Examples are the Police and Criminal Evidence Act 1984, the Terrorism Act 2000 and the Prevention of Terrorism Act 2005. Whilst such statutes may of themselves be controversial[56] (particularly in respect to the role of Police Surgeons),[57] and do curtail the profession's freedom to act autonomously, it is difficult to morally argue that the profession should have the freedom to withhold information about an individual person, when to do so is contrary to the greater interest of wider public safety. One way of looking at such statutes is to consider them as enabling or freeing the profession to legitimately overcome the usual code of professional confidentiality and the Human Rights Act in the interests of society at large, rather than being restrictive of professional activity.

54 JM Consulting, *The Regulation of Nurses, Midwives and Health Visitors. Report on a Review on the Nurses, Midwives and Health Visitors Act 1997* (Bristol: JM Consulting Ltd, 1998) 42.

55 *See* note 52: 52.

56 Q&A: *Terrorism Laws*, BBC News [online], 3 July 2006. Available at: http://news.bbc.co.uk/1/hi/uk_politics/4715478.stm, accessed: 16 October 2010.

57 Association of Police Surgeons & the BMA, *Revised Interim Guidelines on Confidentiality for Police Surgeons in England, Wales and Northern Ireland* (London: BMA, 1998).

CONCLUSION

It would be very easy to name statute after statute and identify how that particular statute affected, for better or for worse, the activities of the medical profession. However, that is not the purpose of this dissertation. The intention of this chapter has been to indicate how statute law can work in favour of, as well as against, the medical profession.

The interesting finding is that some statutes (e.g. the Abortion Act 1967 and the Compensation Act 2006), are developed in support of existing case law and aimed at consolidating the same in support of the established working practices of doctors. Other Acts are brought forth as a direct legislative response to established medical practices that society is no longer willing to tolerate (e.g. the Human Tissue Act 2004), or to facilitate (albeit controversially) the work of doctors in respect to the greater public good (e.g. the Mental Health Acts 1984 and the Prevention of Terrorism Act 2006).

As governments seem reluctant to debate the more controversial ethical issues, perhaps the medical profession can guard against the too frequent imposition of legislation designed to curtail its activities by showing greater sensitivity to the changing nuances within contemporary society. The development of professional standards of practice, sensibly considered guidelines, and codes of conduct should go a long way to ensuring that the need for statutory legislation is kept to a minimum. Where new statutes are deemed necessary, such responsible action by the profession should help to ensure that the legislature takes the already established high standards and well-rehearsed arguments of the profession as its basis for the new laws.

In summary, statute law may presently be of a restrictive nature as well as offering certain freedoms. However, by working in a medico-legally perspicacious manner, the medical profession can go a long way to influencing statute law to its own advantage. At least in respect to this area of law, there is no reason for the medical profession to feel unnecessarily fettered, except perhaps by its own indiscriminate volition.

Chapter 8

The 21st-century perspective

'All changed; changed utterly.'[1]

'Easter, 1916', WB Yeats

'You know my views about some regulations – they're written for the obedience of fools and the guidance of wise men.'[2]

Harry Day to Douglas Bader, 1931

THE 21ST-CENTURY DOCTOR MIGHT BE FORGIVEN FOR BELIEVING the profession to be less autonomous and more greatly fettered by the law than at any other time in the history of the profession.

For many doctors, the advancement and demands of enhanced professional regulation in the early part of the 21st century[3] are the cause of significant unrest; perhaps, as Catto has pointed out, because

1 WB Yeats, *Collected Poems* (London: The Folio Society, 2007) 215.
2 Susan Ratcliffe, editor, *The Oxford Dictionary of Thematic Quotations* (Oxford: Oxford University Press, 2000) 217.5.
3 Carol Black, Advancing 21st-century medical professionalism, *JAMA*, 2009; 301(20): 2156.

of this perceived loss of autonomy.[4] However, for doctors not to grasp the need to reform professional regulation would arguably increase the loss of autonomy and freedom from the level currently enjoyed and risk becoming 'a political disaster'.[5] Witness the words of Lord Phillips:

> [E]xternal regulatory dependence implacably leads to a rising mass of codified petty regulation, swollen by the need for rules to enforce rules and to counter their avoidance. The very equality of treatment such regulatory complexity is nobly designed to ensure, in fact makes it impossible. What is more, state regulation in such areas is apt to drive out self-policing and the force of individual conscience.[6]

Indeed (although the public perception of doctors having independence from government interference may not be quite as strong with the introduction of GP Commissioning in 2013),[7] there may be additional merit in the view that: 'there must be [a] substantial risk that public confidence in the independence of their doctors is undermined if patients believe them to be under state control.'[8] Not quite as an aside, the very subject of GP Commissioning (noted above) is of great interest in respect to the topic of this dissertation, as the government has chosen to call its white paper *Equality and Excellence: liberating the NHS*.[9] The implication here is that, as a result of the changes in how services are commissioned, medical practitioners

---

4 Sir Graeme Catto, The profession in the 21st century, *West Indian Med J*, 2007; 56: 3.

5 Mike Pringle, Regulation and revalidation of doctors, *BMJ*, 2006; 333: 162.

6 Lord Phillips, quoted in: Sir Graeme Catto, The profession in the 21st century, *West Indian Med J*, 2007; 56: 3.

7 Henry Featherstone, GP Commissioning will be good for patients and the NHS, *The Spectator*, 13 July 2010, available at: www.spectator.co.uk/coffeehouse/6140998/gp-commissioning-will-be-good-for-patients-and-the-nhs.thtml, accessed: 26 October 2010.

8 James Johnson, in: Will we be getting good doctors and safer patients? *BMJ*, 2007; 334: 451.

9 Department of Health, *Equality and Excellence: liberating the NHS* (London: HMSO, 2010).

(at least in respect to general medical practitioners) will have greater freedom in this particular field of their practice than at present.

Professional regulation is, of course, nothing new. It might be said that, within the United Kingdom, regulation has been around for the past 150 years, since the formation of the General Medical Council.[10] However, the reality is that regulation has been around far longer than that, as the discussion in Chapter 3 showed in relation to the situation in 15th-century England, and even further back in time if Ancient Persia is brought into consideration. Nonetheless, what was deemed to be appropriate regulation six centuries ago (or even one generation ago) is no longer appropriate for the modern era; as society changes, so too must the standards doctors adopt as the hallmark of their professionalism if the trust of the public is to be maintained.[11] In other words, it might be argued that professionals need to be prepared to reinvent their profession every few generations. Indeed, the present need for reform of medical regulation had been internationally recognised long before the Shipman inquiry[12] (although it is perhaps astonishing that, up until as recently as July 2000, the registration of a doctor in the United Kingdom would not have been affected by a criminal conviction abroad).[13]

First established under the Medical Act 1858, the GMC remains the primary statutory body for the registration and regulation of medical practitioners[14] and, as from 1 April 2010 following the merger of the Postgraduate Medical Education and Training Board with the GMC, for all medical education in the United Kingdom.[15] Its purpose has

10 Sir Graeme Catto, The profession in the 21st century, *West Indian Med J*, 2007; 56: 3.

11 Jeffrey Braithwaite, New professionalism in the 21st century, *Lancet*, 2006; 367: 645.

12 The International Association of Medical Regulatory Authorities (IAMRA) was formed in 2000, following biennial international conferences on medical regulation since 1994. Available at: www.iamra.com, accessed: 23 October 2010.

13 Leslie Keegan, Giving doctors the right treatment, *The Lawyer*, 21 August 2000. Available at: www.thelawyer.com/giving-doctors-the-right-treatment/104727.article, accessed: 23 October 2010.

14 General Medical Council, *The Role of the GMC*, available at: www.gmc-uk.org/about/role.asp, accessed: 23 October 2010.

15 General Medical Council, *Creating a Single Regulator for Medical Education*, available at: www.gmc-uk.org/education/postgraduate/merger.asp, accessed: 23 October 2010.

been defined by various legislation, the most recent being the Medical Act 1983. However, the complexity of this legislation, and thereby the complexity of the law relating to any doctor practising in the 21st century, is demonstrated by the opening paragraph of the Medical Act 1983 in its current form with amendments:[16]

> Medical Act 1983 (as amended by the Professional Performance Act 1995,[17] the European Primary Medical Qualifications Regulations 1996,[18] the NHS (Primary Care) Act 1997,[19] the Medical Act (Amendment) Order 2000,[20] the Medical Act 1983 (Provisional Registration) Regulations 2000,[21] the Medical Act 1983 (Amendment) Order 2002,[22] the National Health Service Reform and Health Care Professionals Act 2002,[23] The European Qualifications (Health Care Professions) Regulations 2003, The European Qualifications

16 General Medical Council, *Medical Act 1983 (consolidated version with amendments)*, available at: www.gmc-uk.org/about/legislation/medical_act.asp, accessed: 23 October 2010.

17 The Professional Performance Act 1995 provided the GMC with additional powers to discipline a doctor whose 'standard of professional performance . . . is found . . . to have been seriously deficient' and not just when there is deemed to have been 'serious professional misconduct'.

18 Under the European Primary Medical Qualifications Regulations 1996, the GMC is required to take into account any experience or training acquired in another Member State when considering applications for registration by European Economic Area (EEA) nationals (or others with enforceable EC rights).

19 The NHS (Primary Care) Act 1997 provided the regulations to primary care trusts in respect to the setting up of Pilot Schemes in respect to Personal Dental Services.

20 The Medical Act (Amendment) Order 2000 widened the powers of the GMC to enable it to act swiftly and effectively when a doctor's fitness to practise is called into question.

21 Medical Act 1983 (Provisional Registration) Regulations 2000 allowed for nationals of an EEA state to be provisionally registered for the purpose of acquiring clinical experience required for a primary European qualification, and for the purpose of obtaining clinical experience once qualified but prior to full registration.

22 The Medical Act 1983 (Amendment) Order 2002 reformed the size and function of the GMC in order to 'provide better protection and improved safeguards for the public; . . . clearer and more straightforward procedures in relation to fitness to practise which are in the interests of both the medical profession and the public at large; and . . . greater accountability and transparency around the working of the GMC itself' (*per* Lord Hunt, address to the House of Lords, Hansard, HL Deb 3 December 2002, 641, cols. 1098–112).

23 The NHS Reform and Health Care Professions Act 2002 provided for the establishment of NHS Foundation Trusts, the Independent Regulator (Monitor), the Healthcare Commission (Commission for Healthcare Audit and Inspection [CHAI]) and the Commission for Social Care Inspection (CSCI). It abolished the National Care Standards Commission and the Commission for Health Improvement (CHI).

(Health & Social Care Professions and Accession of new Member States) Regulations 2004, the Medical Act 1983 (Amendment) and Miscellaneous Amendments Order 2006, and The European Qualifications (Health and Social Care Professions) Regulations 2007[24]).

There can be no doubt that a significant cause of the scale of reform now taking place in respect to the regulation of the medical profession in the 21st century has been as a direct result of *Shipman*[25] and the inquiry that followed.[26] The proposals for reform were initially discussed in the Chief Medical Officer's 2006 review, *Good Doctors, Safer Patients*,[27] and subsequently encapsulated in the government's 2007 white paper, *Trust, Assurance and Safety – The Regulation of Health Professionals in the 21st Century*.[28] However, many authors have expressed concerns regarding the magnitude of the changes proposed; none least so than the change in the burden of proof[29] from a criminal standard of proof ('beyond reasonable doubt')[30] to a civil standard of proof ('balance of probability')[31] when the GMC is dealing with allegations against doctors.[32] Although a 'sliding scale' of evidence has been suggested,[33] with more serious issues requiring a higher burden of proof, some commentators have predicted that

24 Several of the amendments cited relate to the need to recognise the qualifications of medical professionals from the EEA in accordance with EU Directive 2005/36/EC.

25 *R v Dr Harold Shipman* (1999) – *The Shipman Enquiry* (London: Department of Health, 2002). Available at: www.the-shipman-inquiry.org.uk/home.asp, accessed: 16 October 2010.

26 Dr Peter Schutte, *MDU examines post-Shipman reforms*, available at: www.the-mdu.com/search/hidden_Article.asp?articleID=1648&contentType=Media+release&articleTitle=MDU+examines+post-Shipman+reforms&userType=, accessed: 23 October 2010.

27 Liam Donaldson, *Good Doctors, Safer Patients* (London: Department of Health, 2006).

28 *Trust, Assurance and Safety – The Regulation of Health Professionals in the 21st Century*, available at: www.official-documents.gov.uk/document/cm70/7013/7013.pdf, accessed 23 October 2010.

29 Ibid.: 4, 4.3, 59.

30 AP Simester and GR Sullivan, *Criminal Law Theory and Doctrine*, 3rd ed. (Oxford: Hart, 2007) 54.

31 Ibid.: 59.

32 Clare Dyer, Doctors lose power to regulate their profession, *BMJ*, 2007; 334: 389.

33 *Trust, Assurance and Safety*, 4, 4.8, 60.

doctors will see this as a violation of their rights when their professional reputation and livelihood are threatened.[34] It is possible that it might even represent a breach of Article 6[35] of the Human Rights Act 1998;[36] although the possibility that the GMC might introduce 'plea bargaining'[37] (whereby, in respect to 'minor' cases, conditions might be attached to a doctor's registration without a hearing) may help to offset the perception of personal affront. Nonetheless, as one barrister has stated: 'Whilst there may be an argument for retaining the criminal standard of proof in misconduct cases, the argument for retaining this in cases which involve judgments concerning standards of professional performance or in relation to the health of a doctor, seem very weak.'[38] As part of the process of regulatory reform stemming from the paper *Trust, Assurance and Safety*, all doctors from 2012,[39] are required to undergo a five-yearly process of revalidation (consisting of annual licensing and strengthened annual appraisal leading to five-yearly recertification) in order to maintain their name on the medical register. Failure to complete the process will mean that they will not be able to practise. Signalling the firm intent to move forwards with the process of revalidation, Parliament debated the draft Responsible Officer Regulations[40] and, with their

34 David Bruce, Regulation of doctors, *BMJ*, 2007; 334: 436.

35 Article 6 of the Human Rights Act 1998 provides for the right to a fair trial.

36 Ash Samanta and Jo Samanta, Safer patients and good doctors: medical regulation in the 21st century, *Clin Risk*, 2007; 13: 139.

37 Clare Dyer, GMC to introduce 'plea bargaining' for less serious misconduct cases, *BMJ*, 2007; 334, 763.

38 Leslie Keegan, Giving doctors the right treatment, *The Lawyer*, 21 August 2000. Available at: www.thelawyer.com/giving-doctors-the-right-treatment/104727.article, accessed: 23 October 2010.

39 General Medical Council, *Revalidation date set for 2012*, Press Release, available at: www.gmc-uk.org/news/8054.asp, accessed: 23 October 2010.

40 The draft Responsible Officer Regulations were laid before Parliament on 26 July 2010. The Responsible Officers will oversee the local annual appraisal process and make the five-yearly recommendation to the GMC as to whether a doctor should be revalidated.

controversial[41] passage through the House of Lords,[42] these became effective from 1 January 2011.[43]

However, rather than have the process seen as officious in its nature, the Royal College of General Practitioners prefers to consider it as a matter of professional development.[44] This view is shared by the GMC: 'Revalidation is something that the public expect their doctors to undertake and, if implemented sensitively and effectively, is something that will support all doctors in their innate professional desire to improve their practice still further.'[45] This view of what some would call the 'greatest change to the regulation of the medical profession in 150 years'[46] is not shared by all doctors, as many see revalidation as a threat[47] or 'too complicated and aspirational'.[48] Nonetheless, it is a process which is considered essential if the profession is to redefine its 'contract with society'.[49]

The 21st-century doctor may consider that the obligation to undertake this aforementioned revision is new and onerous; onerous it may indeed be, but new it is not. A review of history suggests that the medical profession's response to the considerable changes occurring

41 The House of Lords debated the legislation on 23 November 2010. Some Lords felt that the Regulations were premature in view of uncertainty with the process of revalidation and where Responsible Officers will sit once the primary care trusts are abolished in 2013. The transcript from the debate can be accessed at: Hansard, House of Lords debates, www.publications.parliament.uk/pa/ld201011/ldhansrd/text/101123-0002.htm#10112348000093, accessed: 26 November 2010.

42 Gareth Iacobucci, Responsible officers roll out gets green light, *Pulse*, 26 Nov 2010, available at: www.pulsetoday.co.uk/story.asp?storycode=4127885&cid=Latest_headlines_2_261110&sp_rid=NjU3NzMzMDg0MgS2&sp_mid=36027162, accessed: 26 November 2010.

43 General Medical Council, *Response to our revalidation consultation* (London: GMC, October 2010) 19.

44 Steve Field, Revalidation still moving forward, says RCGP Chair, *RCGP News*, 2010; July: 1.

45 General Medical Council, *Revalidation: a statement of intent* (London: GMC, October 2010) 1.

46 Mike Pringle, Revalidation: clearer and closer, *Br J Gen Pract*, 2010; July: 475.

47 Fiona Godlee, Concerns about revalidation, *BMJ*, 2006; 333: 966.

48 Clare Dyer, Plans for revalidation are 'too complicated and aspirational', *BMJ*, 2010; 341: 854.

49 William M Sullivan, Medicine under threat: professionalism and professional identity, *CMAJ*, 2000; 162(5): 675.

with the industrialisation of society between the mid 18th century and the end of the 19th century was the 'gradual institution of reform and improvement'.[50] It may well be that the profession of today cannot avoid one author's prediction that the 21st century is heralding 'a new era of managerialist intervention by government, moving away from the traditional paradigm of professional autonomy and self-regulation',[51] and that the 'tightening of centralised control of professional practice'[52] by the state is a 'modern day reality'.[53] However, it is possible that in time historical analysis of these 21st-century events will demonstrate that the medical profession once again metamorphosed and found, by a process of strengthened regulation, a way to reaffirm the value of professional autonomy as 'an essential component of high quality medical care'.[54]

The medical profession must achieve the latter before the law brings it about on the behalf of medicine. That said, it does not have to be an adversarial course of events. Although there is a recognised 'basic tension'[55] between the two professions, and on some subjects (such as on the subject of evidence) there is a 'discrepancy of understanding'[56] between medicine and law, at the end of the first decade of the 21st century (and almost six hundred years since Henry V first applied the law to the practising of medicine) it remains true that: 'when physicians and lawyers work together they can be a much more powerful influence on society than when they act separately or simple advocate for their own self-interest'.[57] That there is such a symbiotic

50 Dorothy Parker, Medicine and industrial society: reform, improvement and professionalization, *Victorian Stud*, 1993; 37(1): 129.

51 A Davies, Don't trust me, I'm a doctor, *Oxf J Leg Stud*, 2000; 20: 444.

52 David Price, *Legal Aspects of the Regulation of the Health Professions*. In: Judith Allsop and Mike Saks, editors, *Regulating the Health Professions* (London: Sage, 2002) 60.

53 Ibid.

54 The World Medical Association, *Declaration of Madrid on Professional Autonomy and Self-Regulation*, [1987] 2005. Available at: www.wma.net/en/30publications/10policies/a21/index.html, accessed: 14 October 2009.

55 John M Eisenberg, What does evidence mean? Can the law and medicine be reconciled? *J Health Polit Policy Law*, 2001; 26(2): 381.

56 Ibid.: 374.

57 George J Annas, The art of medicine: doctors and lawyers and wolves, *Lancet*, 2008; 371: 1833.

relation between the two professions can be seen even with today's regulatory changes. Whilst the various Acts, Orders and Regulations ushered in between 1995 and 2006 to amend the Medical Act 1983 have largely been necessitated by society's requirement for greater regulation of doctors, the fact remains that many of the statutes are lacking in detail. It is as though the law is dictating to medicine that change must happen; however, the way that the change is brought about has been left largely to the deliberations of the medical profession itself. The process of revalidation is a good case in point, whereby the mechanism for the formalised control of professional standards of practice has been delegated by the legislature to the GMC and royal medical colleges to determine between them: professional medical autonomy rules, albeit within the boundaries set, as ever, by the law.

CONCLUSION

The 21st century has heralded one of the biggest changes in medical regulation since the creation of the General Medical Council 150 years ago. Arguably, it is the greatest change since the practice of medicine was formally recognised as a fledgling profession in the time of the Tudors. The recent suggestion that 'regulation is a dynamic process'[58] becomes self-evident when the debates and reforms of the past decade or so are considered. However, the statement gains even more credence when the process of regulation is viewed over many centuries. History informs us that change happens, and in this respect, the current process of regulatory reform is not really new; the scale of it is just larger than anything those of us practising today have previously experienced.

On this occasion, the regulatory reformation has been predominantly driven by the demands of society, on the background of

58 Graeme Catto, Will we be getting good doctors and safer patients?, *BMJ*, 2007; 334: 450.

informed voices from within the medical profession. Its initiation, however, has been a legal process; the stipulations of society have prompted an enabling legislative process, with new Acts, Orders and Regulations, against which the input of the medical profession has been set.

There is, nonetheless, a salutary lesson to be taken from this process.

Harry Day's view was that 'regulations are for the guidance of wise men' (noted in the epigraph). If that view is subscribed to, it might be suggested that it is an even wiser man who takes the lead in formulating the rules in the first place. Regulatory reform is therefore one significant example where medicine must work in close liaison with the law if the former is not to be dominated by the latter. The needs of society are better met if the two professions work in tandem. It can be argued that this is indeed the process that has been adopted: Parliament has laid down the legislative process, which the medical profession is now using as the guidance for its own permutation of reform through the GMC and the royal colleges.

The words of WB Yeats, 'All changed; changed utterly', may ring very true for doctors at the start of the 21st century. However, as the GMC has stated, 'revalidation should add value for both patients and doctors'.[59] If the law is indeed used as medicine's friend, and is not treated as the profession's nemesis, then, as the doctor and author AJ Cronin predicted when referring to the uncertain process of change, 'a door will open for us . . . one that will ultimately prove good for us'.[60] In which case, the next line of Yeats' poem may also ring true: 'A terrible beauty is born'.[61]

59 General Medical Council, *Response to our revalidation consultation* (London: GMC, October 2010) 4.

60 AJ Cronin, quoted in: Spencer Johnson, *Who Moved My Cheese?* (Reading: Vermilion, 1999) 9.

61 WB Yeats, 'Easter, 1916', *Collected Poems* (London: The Folio Society, 2007) 215.

Chapter 9

Conclusion

THIS BOOK WAS PLANNED IN ORDER TO EXAMINE THE INTER-relationship between law and medicine from an historic perspective. As a preliminary premise, it was hypothesised that the unregulated and unqualified 'quacks' of the era prior to the 16th century, with their medications and therapies of little proven value, had a freedom and level of autonomy which, paradoxically, has subsequently been denied the modern medical professional, despite the latter's access to a superior level of education, greater knowledge and advanced science. It was initially my personal belief that, through a process of regulatory reform, ever-developing case law and the enactment of successive primary legislation by Parliament, the law might be seen as having, somewhat irresolutely, turned the autonomous and, at times, infamous quack into a modern, highly intelligent, but significantly fettered, professional. In essence, this dissertation commenced with the perception that the law was, in respect to medicine, open to the charge of being a meddlesome and inhibitory power, and most certainly to be treated as an adversary. The introduction to this dissertation laid out the aforementioned concept and set down the process by which it was hoped to show that an alternative view was in truth not only possible but more accurately a defining reality.

In the first two chapters, some of the more philosophical aspects underlying the existence of the two professions were considered alongside a gentle probing into the meaning behind the terms 'autonomy', 'freedom' and 'rights', especially in respect to the significant place of the Kantian principle of autonomy within modern healthcare ethics, Cicero and Rousseau's insights to the notion of freedom, and the permeation of civil, constitutional and human rights into modern Western law. The juxtaposition of all of these factors with the two professions of law and medicine was considered in relation to the concept of society, and the conclusion drawn that the relationship between medicine and society is, and has to be by virtue of medicine's very raison d'être, a symbiotic one. It was suggested that, as a result, the belief that doctors can be (or ever were) really autonomous is a fallacy, with freedom being a perception grounded in relativity, and medicine as a profession indubitably exposed to the general will of society.

Consideration of the relationship between medicine, law and society was continued on a more specific basis within Chapter 3. It was recognised that society cannot itself exist without the existence of laws, and therefore that there is an inevitable intermeshing of law and medicine through the complex medium of society. Nonetheless, as an interesting, and not entirely irrelevant aside, it was also noted that for a few writers (both academics and playwrights amongst them), medicine may itself be considered to be a nemesis in respect to modern society. In this respect, the law might be seen as society's benevolent agent in restraining what is perceived, by some, to be the more malevolent aspects of medicine's influence on society. Related to this, the discussion in Chapter 3 also considered the nature of what a profession is, along with what being a professional entails, and debated the concept that medicine (and primary care in particular) might best be 'deprofessionalised' in the enhanced interests of society. The conclusion ultimately drawn was that there exist several dichotomies, none of which can be harmoniously resolved without detriment to another aspect of the equation: society needs both law and medicine, but by befriending medicine, there is a danger that the law may be undermining its very purpose in providing the infrastructure for society. However, by having due regard and consideration to its primary, cultural master, law may in turn be accused of making medicine an opponent. Ultimately, the libertarian perspective of Mills offered the compromise of collaboration between the three interested parties on agreed terms of whatever constituted mutual best interests.

The ancient historical perspective regarding the relationship between doctors and the law was outlined in Chapter 4. It was noted that the need for the regulation of doctors was recognised by none other than Hippocrates; so perhaps those of the present generation of doctors quietly fearing the process of revalidation may be heartened by the possibility that it is something which has arguably taken not 10 years, but 1710 years to bring to fruition!

On a more serious note, it was shown that regulatory control and legal remedies existed in parts of the world almost as far back as four thousand years ago. However, although the Romans influenced the situation in England to some extent, the significant movement away from unregulated quackery was not made until the time of King Henry V, and even more so with King Henry VIII. Indeed, although the phrase 'from time immemorial' relates to the time of the death of King Henry II (6 July 1189), with courts discounting all legal transactions which occurred prior to that date,[1] then, if that is the start of 'legal memory', 'medico-legal memory' was a late developer. Indeed, 'medico-legal memory' might be deemed to run from the reign of his distant successor Henry VIII, who introduced several 16th-century regulatory Acts for the medical profession, albeit more in respect to curtailing the activities of the quacks than restricting the educated physicians. An examination of case law contemporaneous to that period certainly indicated that, for the 16th and 17th-century physician, the law was, with a few notable exceptions, a welcomed and benign acquaintance.

It has been demonstrated in the course of Chapter 5 that the evolution of the general medical practitioner, prompted by an important

1 Geoffrey Rivlin, *Understanding the Law*, 4th ed. (Oxford: Oxford University Press, 2006) 23.

piece of case law in the form of *William Rose v College of Physicians*, was a significant turning point in the 18th century, followed by the equally important Apothecaries Act of 1815. The irony, however, was that although the law at this latter time was the nemesis of the unqualified quacks and a friend to the newly emerged general medical practitioners, its actions were concomitantly unfavourable to the existing physicians. Nonetheless, it is at this stage that the law is seen to be acting in the best interests of the society it serves, rather than appeasing the medical profession in its entirety. The physicians may well have felt the loss of autonomy. However, for the apothecary-turned-general-practitioner, the newly found ability to practise freed from the chains of the physicians brought a new sense of autonomy, as well as greater degree of benevolence for the population of 19th-century society.

The impact of the common law on the practice of medicine was examined within Chapter 6. The chapter opened with Alexander Pope's question as to 'who shall decide when doctors disagree?' The evidence suggests that, when it comes to the more difficult moral and ethical issues, it is the common law which initially points the way, with Parliament often taking a spectator role for the early stages of any major controversial issues. It was highlighted that this stance has often caused concern amongst the law lords, especially in relation to matters such as the withholding of life-prolonging treatment (e.g. *Burke and Airedale NHS Trust v Bland*) and assisted suicide (*Pretty*).

Nonetheless, an analysis of common law cases involving the right to refuse consent to treatment (e.g. *Re T*), matters of capacity to consent (e.g. *Re MB*), claims for medical negligence (e.g. *Bolam* and *Bolitho*), the issue of consent (e.g. *Sidaway*), informed consent (e.g. *Chester* and *Gregg*), and the capacity of young people to consent to treatment (e.g. *Gillick*), all showed that the courts often serve a most useful purpose in teasing out the moral and ethical arguments in addition to the facts of law. Arguments which then usefully serve to inform the future action of the medical profession. Indeed, such cases have often been considered by judges (Lord Denning and Lord

Donaldson in particular) who have openly expressed the desire that the law should not adversely constrain the benevolent actions of the medical profession and should, where possible, seek to protect the profession from unnecessary or undesirable attacks in law.

Notwithstanding the above, the common law has also demonstrated its willingness to take a more critical view of doctors who have overstepped the accepted legal boundaries or wandered into uncertain ethical territory without first seeking a legal opinion. The conclusion to Chapter 6 emphasised this point and suggested that the answer to Alexander Pope's question was most certainly such that, not only has the common law demonstrated its ability and willingness to decide on appropriate courses of action when doctors are presented with controversial ethical dilemmas, it has clearly reserved the pre-eminent right to do so. In essence, through the process of the common law, the law has declared its willingness to act as an accommodating accomplice to the medical profession, albeit under a strict understanding of the terms of the relationship.

The impact of statute law on the practice of medicine was the subject of Chapter 7, with the chapter's opening statistics indicating just how influential this aspect of law is on the practice of medicine. From the examples discussed, there can be no doubt that statute law serves as an important controlling authority in respect to how the medical profession functions in relation to the society it serves (e.g. the Mental Health Act 1983 and the Abortion Act 1967). However, it is a two-edged sword, with some Acts functioning to protect the integrity of the practice of medicine as a profession (e.g. the Apothecaries Act 1815 and the Medical Act 1858), whilst other Acts seek to establish control over areas of medical activity that society has heretofore not appreciated took place or that modern society has found distasteful (e.g. the Human Tissue Act 2004). It is also clear that a number of Acts have been developed (at least in part) from established case law (e.g. the Mental Capacity Act 2005), thereby emphasising the important role the common law serves in shaping the government's perspective as to how medicine should relate to society. The views of the medical profession have invariably been heard in the course of such litigious court room debates, and are usually sought again by parliamentary committees during the process of drafting the related Acts, thus ensuring that doctors have considerable opportunity in shaping the laws which in turn shape their professional destiny.

The discussion on statute law also outlined the need for, and the considerable value of, enhanced regulation within the medical profession, both in respect to the standards doctors portray to society and to the activities carried out purportedly on behalf of society. The suggestion is that the development, regular remodelling and careful enforcement of professional standards can go a long way towards preserving a degree of autonomous professional activity, thereby avoiding too-frequent intervention by the law in its guise as society's moderator. Chapter 7 concluded that, acting with wisdom and perspicacity, the medical profession can work in a symbiotic manner with the law, thereby ensuring that statute law appertaining to the practice of medicine worked in a protective and supportive manner, without being overly restrictive or dogmatic.

Chapter 8 brought the discussion up to date with consideration of the medico-legally momentous events unfolding within the first decade of the 21st century, with a reconsideration of the nature of professional regulation being the central core of the debates. However, although the changes being brought about as part of this process (e.g. licensing, revalidation and the change in emphasis in respect to the burden of proof required by the GMC from the criminal standard to the civil standard) may be seen as draconian by a few doctors, intrusive by some and of a professional inconvenience by many, there can be no doubt that, taken in the wider context, they are simply an extension of the process first postulated by Hippocrates, modelled by Tudor law, legally adjusted and enhanced during the 17th and 18th centuries, and reaffirmed by various statutes, case law and regulatory processes of the 19th and 20th centuries.

This book set out to examine the relationship between law and medicine from an historic perspective. The suggestion was that, as the value of medicine to society has increased through greater knowledge and scientific advances, the autonomous activity of those purporting to purvey the skills such knowledge demands has been progressively transformed and eroded; that the freedoms initially enjoyed by unqualified quacks have been regulated and legislated for and against, thereby transforming the quack into a highly constrained, modern-day medical professional for whom the concept of autonomy is but a relative value. The truth, however, is not that simple. An evaluation of the interaction of law and medicine has, it is suggested, indicated that whilst the law serves to formulate the boundaries within which society expects its doctors to practise, the integrity of medical practice as a profession is also securely protected by law, and that within those sheltered boundaries, doctors continue to enjoy a considerable degree of professional autonomy. It might be said that, with the expected establishment of primary care commissioning in 2013, this is particularly the case for the 21st-century general medical practitioner; a branch of the profession which has travelled a long way since the Apothecaries Act of 1815.

Law and medicine are both implicit servants to the society in which the two professions exist. Whilst still allowing considerable autonomy, and not exactly fettering the medical professional, the law serves to protect, moderate, control and influence the activities of the medical profession. In the words of Sir Cyril Chantler: 'Medicine used to be simple, ineffective and relatively safe. Now it is complex, effective and potentially dangerous.'[2] Perhaps it is therefore correct that the relationship between law and medicine should be thus so.

2 Cyril Chantler, The role and education of doctors in the delivery of health care, *Lancet*, 1999; 353: 1178–81.

Bibliography

BOOKS

Adams F. *The Genuine Works of Hippocrates translated from the Greek*. Florida: Krieger Publishing Company; [1849] 1972.

Adler MJ. *The Idea of Freedom*. New York: Doubleday; 1958.

Allsop J, Saks M. *Regulating the Health Professions*. London: Sage Publications; 2002.

Aufderheide AC. *The Scientific Study of Mummies*. Cambridge: Cambridge University Press; 2003.

Baker C, editor. *Ernest Hemingway: selected letters 1917–1961*. New York: Scribner Book Company; 2003.

Bartlett P, Sandland R. *Mental Health Law*. 3rd ed. Oxford: Oxford University Press; 2007.

Beauchamp TL, Childress JF. *Principles of Biomedical Ethics*. 6th ed. Oxford: Oxford University Press; 2009.

Berger J. *A Fortunate Man: the story of a country doctor*. New York: Vintage; [1967] 1997.

Brazier M, Cave E. *Medicine, Patients and the Law*. 4th ed. London: Penguin; 2007.

Cane P. *Atiyah's Accidents, Compensation and the Law*. 7th ed. Cambridge: Cambridge University Press; 2006.

Card R. *Criminal Law*. 18th ed. Oxford: Oxford University Press; 2008.

Cawthon E. *Medicine on Trial: a sourcebook with cases*. California: ABC-CLIO Inc; 2004.

Churchill WS. *The Dawn of Liberation*. London: Cassell; 1944.

Cole GDH, translator. *Great Books*, Vol. 35. Chicago, IL: Encyclopaedia Britannica; [1952] 1990.

Cope Z. *The Worshipful Society of Apothecaries of London and the Evolution of the Family Doctor*. London: The Society of Apothecaries; c. 1967.

Corfield L, Granne E, Latimer-Sayer W. *ABC of Medical Law*. Oxford: Wiley-Blackwell; 2009.

Cronin AJ. *The Citadel*. London: Victor Gollancz; 1937.

Davies M. *Medical Law*. 2nd ed. Oxford: Oxford University Press; [1996] 1998.

Denning, Lord. *The Discipline of Law*. Oxford: Oxford University Press; 1979.

Devlin P. *Easing the Passing: the trial of Dr John Bodkin Adams*. London: Bodley Head; 1985.

Digby A. *The Evolution of British General Practice 1850–1948*. Oxford: Oxford University Press; 1999.

Donne J. Meditation XVII, Nunc Lento Sonitu Dicunt Morieris, from Devotions upon Emergent Occasions (1623). In: Walton I, editor. *John Donne, Devotions upon Emergent Occasions and Death's Duel*. New York: Vintage Books; 1999.

English V, Romano-Critchley G, Sheather J, Sommerville A. *Medical Ethics Today*. 2nd ed. London: BMJ Books; [1993] 2004.

Forbes J, Tweedie A, Conolly J, editors. *The Cyclopaedia of Practical Medicine*. London: Sherwood, Gilbert and Piper; 1835.

Fry J, Lord Hunt of Fawley, Pinsent RJFH, editors. (1983) *A History of the Royal College of General Practitioners: the first 25 years*. Lancaster: MTP Press; 1983.

Gabe J, Calnan M, Bury M, editors. *The Sociology of the Health Service*. New York: Routledge; 1991.

George III (by Command of). *The Statutes of the Realm*. London: The Record Commission; 1817.

Giesen D. *International Medical Malpractice Law*. Boston, MA: Kluwer Academic Publishers; 1988.

Given-Wilson C, editors. *The Parliament Rolls of Medieval England, 1275–1504*. (CD-ROM). Leicester: Scholarly Digital Editions; 2005.

Harpwood V. *Medicine, Malpractice and Misapprehensions*. Oxford: Routledge Cavendish; 2007.

Herbert AP. *Uncommon Law*. Kelly Bray: House of Stratus; [1935] 2001.

Herring J. *Criminal Law, Text, Cases, and Materials*. 3rd ed. Oxford: Oxford University Press; 2006.

Honderich T, editor. *The Oxford Companion to Philosophy*. Oxford: Oxford University Press; 1995.

Hostettler J, Braby R. *Sir William Garrow*. Hampshire: Waterside Press; 2010.

Hunting P. *A History of the Society of Apothecaries*. London: The Society of Apothecaries; 1998.

Illich I. *Limits to Medicine. Medical Nemesis: the expropriation of health*. London: Marion Boyars Publishing; [1995] 2002.

Jackson E. *Medical Law*. Oxford: Oxford University Press; 2006.

Johnson S. *Johnson's Dictionary*. London: Knapton, Longman & Co; 1755.

Johnson S. *Who Moved My Cheese?* Reading: Vermilion; 1999.

Johnston D. *Roman Law in Context*. Cambridge: Cambridge University Press; 1999.

Jones MA. *Medical Negligence*. 4th ed. London: Sweet & Maxwell; 2008.

Jones MA, Morris AE. *Blackstone's Statutes on Medical Law*. 4th ed. Oxford: Oxford University Press; 2005.

Kant I. Fundamental principles of the metaphysic of morals (1785). In: Adler MJ, editor. *Great Books of the Western World*. 2nd ed. Chicago: Encyclopaedia Britannica Inc; [1952] 1990.

Kay C, Roberts J, Samuels M, Wotherspoon I, editors. *Historical Thesaurus of the Oxford English Dictionary*, Vol. 1. Oxford: Oxford University Press; 2009.

Kennedy I, Grubb A. *Medical Law*. 3rd ed. London: Butterworths; 2000.

King A. *The British Constitution*. Oxford: Oxford University Press; 2007.

King LW, translator. *The Code of Hammurabi*. Sioux Falls, SD: NuVision Publications; [1915] 2007.

Knowles E, editor. *The Oxford Dictionary of Quotations*. 5th ed. Oxford: Oxford University Press; 1999.

Kuhse H, Singer P, editors. *A Companion to Bioethics*. Oxford: Blackwell; [1998] 2001.

Larson MS. *The Rise of Professionalism: a sociological analysis*. London: University of California Press; 1977.

Locke J. *Two Treatises of Government*, London: Awnsham Churchill; 1689.

Loudon I. *Medical Care and the General Medical Practitioner 1750–1850*. Oxford: Clarendon Press; 1986.

Loudon I, Horder J, Webster C, editors. *General Practice under the National Health Service 1948–1997*. Oxford: Clarendon Press; 1998.

Margotta R. *History of Medicine*. London: Octopus Publishing; [1996] 2006.

Marti-Ibanez F. *A Prelude to Medical History*. New York: MD Publications; 1961.

Martin EA, Law J, editors. *Oxford Dictionary of Law*. 6th ed. Oxford: Oxford University Press; [1983] 2006.

Mason JK, Laurie GT. *Law and Medical Ethics*. 7th ed. Oxford: Oxford University Press; 2006.

McLean SAM, editor. *First Do No Harm: law, ethics and healthcare*. Aldershot: Ashgate; 2006.

Mcleod I. *Legal Method*. 6th ed. Basingstoke: Palgrave Macmillan; [1993] 2005.

Metternich, Prince. Mein Politisches Testament. In: Von Klinkowstrom A. *Aus Metternich's Nachgelassenen Papieren*, Vol. 7; 1880.

Morris AE, Jones MA. *Blackstone's Statutes on Medical Law*. 6th ed. Oxford: Oxford University Press; 2009.

Neill A, Ridley A. *The Philosophy of Art: readings ancient and modern*. Maidenhead: McGraw-Hill; 1995.

Newell KW. *Health by the People*. Geneva: World Health Organization; 1975.

Ormerod D. *Smith and Hogan Criminal Law*. 12th ed. Oxford: Oxford University Press; 2008.

Orwell G. *1984*. St Louis, MO: Turtleback Books; [1948] 1999.

Pattinson SD. *Medical Law and Ethics*. London: Sweet & Maxwell; 2006.

Pelling M. *Medical Conflicts in Early Modern London: patronage, physicians and irregular practitioners 1550–1640*. Oxford: Clarendon Press; 2003.

Percy R. 'Anecdotes of the Bar': Learned Apothecary. *The Percy Anecdotes*. Vol. 1. London: Frederick Warne; 1868.

Perkin H. *The Third Revolution: professional elites in the modern world*. London: Routledge; 1996.

Porter R. *Quacks, Fakers and Charlatans in Medicine*. Stroud: Tempus Publishing; [1989] 2003.

Rich BA. *Strange Bedfellows: how medical jurisprudence has influenced medical ethics and medical practice*. New York: Kluwer Academic; 2001.

Rivlin G. *Understanding the Law*. 4th ed. Oxford: Oxford University Press; 2006.

Rousseau JJ. *Du Contract Social ou Principes du Droit Politique*. Amsterdam; Chez Marc; 1762.

Shaw GB. *The Doctor's Dilemma*. Fairfield, IA: 1st World Library Literary Society; [1906] 2004.

Simester AP, Sullivan GR. *Criminal Law Theory and Doctrine*. 3rd ed. Oxford: Hart; 2007.

Simpson JA, Weiner ESC, editors. *The Oxford English Dictionary*. 2nd ed. Oxford: Oxford University Press; [1989] 1991.

Singer P, editor. *A Companion to Ethics*. Oxford: Blackwell Publishing; 1991.

Soanes C, editor. *The Compact Oxford English Dictionary*. 2nd ed. Oxford: Oxford University Press; 2000.

Stauch M, Wheat K, Tingle J. *Text, Cases and Materials on Medical Law*. 3rd ed. Oxford: Routledge Cavendish; 2006.

Teff H. *Reasonable Care*. Oxford: Clarendon Press; 1994.

The Holy Bible, Authorised King James Version.

Tocqueville A de. *Democracy in America*. New York: AS Barnes & Co; [1835] 1838.

Tovey G. *Medical Law*. 1st ed. London: Sweet & Maxwell; 2008.

Wacks R. *Law: a very short introduction*. Oxford: Oxford University Press; 2008.

Wacks R. *Philosophy of Law: a very short introduction.* Oxford: Oxford University Press; 2006.

Wall C. *The London Apothecaries.* London: The Apothecaries Hall; c. 1960.

Weatherford R. *The Implications of Determinism.* London: Routledge; 1991.

Weightman H. *The Medical Practitioners' Legal Guide.* London: Renshaw; 1870.

Wilkins D, editor. *Opera Omnia Seldeni (The Works of John Selden Esq. In Three Volumes).* Clark, NJ: Lawbook Exchange; 2006.

Willcock JW, *The Laws Relating to the Medical Profession.* London: Clarke; 1830.

Zend Avesta, The. Part 1 of 3: The Vendidad. Forgotten Books; [c. 8th Century BCE] 2008.

COURSE TEXTS

De Montfort University. *LLM Module Handbook, Clinical Malpractice 1.* Leicester: De Montfort University; 2008.

De Montfort University. *LLM Module Handbook, Clinical Malpractice 2.* Leicester: De Montfort University; 2008.

De Montfort University. *LLM Module Handbook, Consent and the Incapacitated Patient.* Leicester: De Montfort University; 2009.

De Montfort University. *LLM Module Handbook, Introduction to Health Care Law and Ethics.* Leicester: De Montfort University; 2009.

De Montfort University. *LLM Module Handbook, Mental Health.* Leicester: De Montfort University; 2008.

De Montfort University. *LLM Module Handbook, Philosophy of Healthcare.* Leicester: De Montfort University; 2010.

Marwick A. Introduction to history. In: *An Introduction to the Humanities, The Sixties: mainstream culture and counter-culture.* Milton Keynes: Open University; [1998] 2005.

Marwick A. Rousseau's argument. In: *An Introduction to the Humanities, History, Classicism and Revolution.* Milton Keynes: Open University; [1998] 2005.

CASES (ENGLAND AND WALES)

Airedale NHS Trust v Bland [1993] AC 789

Airedale NHS Trust Respondents v Bland Appellant [1993] 2 WLR 316

B (a child) (Welfare of child: Immunisation) [2003] EWCA Civ 1148

B v An NHS Trust (2002) 152 NLJ 470

Bolam v Friern Hospital Management Committee [1957] 1 WLR 582

Bolitho v City and Hackney Health Authority [1997] 4 All ER 771 9HL

Bonham's Case [1606] 77 ER 646

Burke v GMC [2005] EWCA Civ 1003

Butler v The President of the College of Physicians [1631] 79 ER 823

Chester v Afshar [2004] 4 All ER 58 HL

College of Physicians v Butler [1628] (6 Charles 1)

Doctor Trigg v College of Physicians [1652] 82 ER 751

Dr Laughton v Gardener [1606] 79 ER 104

Gillick v West Norfolk and Wisbech Area Health Authority and the DHSS [1986] AC 112

Gregg v Scott [2005] UKHL 2

Hatcher v Black [1954] The Times, 2 July 1954

Hajgato v London Health Assn [1982] 36 OR 2d 669

Hucks v Cole [1968] 118 NLJ 46

IRC v Maxse [1919] 1 KB 647

R v Adams [1957] Crim LR 365

R v Arthur (1981) The Times, 5 November 1981

R v Lodwig (1990) The Times, 16 March 1990

R (on the application of Pretty) v DPP [2001] UKHL 61

R (on the application of Purdy) v DPP [2009] UKHL 45

Re B (Adult: Refusal of Medical Treatment) [2002] All ER 449

Re F (Mental Patient: Sterilisation) [1990] 2 AC 1

Re S (Adult: Refusal of Treatment) [1992] 3 WLR 806

Re T (Adult: Refusal of Medical Treatment) [1992] 4 All ER 649

Re W (A minor: Medical Treatment) [1992] 4 All ER 627

Roe v Ministry of Health [1954] 2 QB 66

Sidaway v Board of Governors of the Bethlem Royal Hospital and the Maudsley Hospital and Others [1984] QB 493

Sidaway v Board of Governors of the Bethlem Royal Hospital and the Maudsley Hospital [1985] AC 871

The College of Physicians v Rose [1703] 87 ER 806

The Corporation of Physitians v Doctor Tenant for practising of physic [1613] 80 ER 1054

Whitehouse v Jordan [1981] 1 All ER 267, HL

William Rose v The College of Physicians, London [1703] 2 ER 857

CASES (COMMONWEALTH AND OTHER JURISDICTIONS)

Brushett v Cowan [1991] 2 Med LR 271 (Newfoundland, CA)

Cruzan v Director, Missouri Department of Health (1990) 110 S. Ct. 2841, 2859

McFadden v U.S. Fidelity and Guarantee Co 766 So. 2d 20 (Miss. Ct. App. 2000)

Mohr v Williams [1905] 104 NW 12 (Supp. Ct. Minn.)

Morton v William Dixon Ltd 1909 SC 807

State v Hoffman 558 P.2d 602 (Utah 1976)

SUMMARY OF INFORMED CONSENT CASES: JAN 2000–SEPT 2010

1 Under the English jurisdiction

A Health Authority v X (No.1) [2001] EWCA Civ 2014

Al Hamwi v Johnston [2005] EWHC 206 (QB)

B (A Child) v Leeds HA [2001] EWCA Civ 51

B (Consent to Treatment: Capacity), Re [2002] EWHC 429 (Fam)

Bailey v Ministry of Defence [2008] EWCA Civ 883

Barratt v South Manchester University Hospital NHS Trust [2001] (QB) Official Transcript

Birch v University College London Hospital NHS Foundation Trust [2008] EWHC 2237 (QB)

Burton v St Albans & Hemel Hempstead NHS Trust [2002] EWHC 1870 (QB)

Chester v Afshar [2004] 4 All ER 58 HL
G v Central and North West London Mental Health NHS Trust [2007] EWHC 3086 (QB)
Jones v North West SHA [2010] EWHC 178 (QB)
L v West Midlands SHA [2009] EWHC 259 (QB)
Loraine v Wirral University Teaching Hospital NHS Foundation Trust [2008] EWHC 1565 (QB)
M v Mid Yorkshire Hospitals NHS Trust [2005] EWHC 3469 (QB)
Marcic v Royal National Orthopaedic Health Trust [2002] (QB) Official Transcript
Markose v Epsom & St Helier NHS Trust [2004] EWHC 3130 (QB)
Mellor v Sheffield Teaching Hospitals NHS Trust [2004] EWHC 780 (QB)
Monk v PC Harrington Ltd [2008] EWHC 1879 (QB)
Newman v Maurice [2010] EWHC 171 (QB)
Palmer v East and North Hertfordshire NHS Trust [2006] EWHC 1997 (QB)
Peet v Mid Kent Area Healthcare NHS Trust [2001] EWCA Civ 1703
Perrins v Holland [2009] EWHC 1945 (Ch)
Portsmouth NHS Trust v Wyatt [2004] EWHC 2247 (Fam)
Preiss v General Dental Council [2001] UKPC 36
Purver v Winchester and Eastleigh Healthcare NHS Trust [2007] EWHC 34 (QB)
R (on the application of B) v Ashworth Hospital Authority [2005] UKHL 20
R (on the application of Pretty) v DPP [2001] UKHL 61
R (on the application of Quintavalle) v Secretary of State for Health [2002] EWCA Civ 29
R (on the application of Stennett) v Manchester City Council [2002] UKHL 34
R (on the application of Wilkinson) v Responsible Medical Officer Broadmoor Hospital and another [2001] EWCA Civ 1545
Rees v Darlington Memorial Hospital NHS Trust [2003] UKHL 52
Rehman v University College London Hospitals NHS Trust [2004] EWHC 1361 (QB)
RP v Nottingham City Council [2008] EWCA Civ 462

Wyatt v Curtis [2003] EWCA Civ 1779

Yearworth v North Bristol NHS Trust [2009] EWCA Civ 37

2 Under the Scottish jurisdiction

Karling v Purdue [2005] PNLR 13

M's Guardian v Lanarkshire Health Board [2010] CSOH 104

3 In the European Court of Human Rights

Rohde v Denmark (69332/01) (2006) 43 EHRR 17

LEGISLATION (ENGLAND AND WALES)

Abortion Act 1967

Access to Health Records Act 1990

Age of Marriage Act 1929

An Act Concerning Barbers and Surgeons 1540

An Act Concerning Physicians 1523

An Act Concerning Physicians 1540

An Act Concerning Physicians & Surgeons 1512/1513

An Act that persons being not surgeons may minister medicines outwardly 1542

An Act that Surgeons be discharged of Constableshipe and other things 1513/1514

Apothecaries Act 1815

Children and Young Persons Act 1933

Compensation Act 2006

Contagious Diseases Act 1866 (29 & 30 Vict. c. 35)

Copyright Act 1842 (5 & 6 Vict. c. 45)

Corporate Manslaughter and Homicide Act 2007

County Asylums Act 1845

Data Protection Act 1998

Ecclesiastical Licences Act 1533

Family Law Reform Act 1969

Health and Social Care Act 2008

Homicide Act 1957
Human Fertilisation and Embryology Act 1990
Human Fertilisation and Embryology Act 2008
Human Rights Act 1998
Human Tissue Act 2004
International Copyright Act 1852 (15 & 16 Vict. c. 12)
Lunacy Act 1845 (8 & 9 Vict. c. 100)
Lunacy Act 1890
Medical Registration Act 1858
Medical Act 1983
Mental Capacity Act 2005
Mental Deficiency Act 1913
Mental Health Act 1959
Mental Health Act 1983
Mental Health Act 2007
National Health Services Act 1946
National Health Service Reform and Health Care Professionals Act 2002
NHS Act 2006
NHS (Primary Care) Act 1997
Nurses, Midwives and Health Visitors Act 1997
Organ Retention and the Human Tissue Act 2004
Peter's Pence Act 1533
Police and Criminal Evidence Act 1984
Poor Law Act 1835
Poor Law Amendment Act 1834
Poor Law Amendment Act 1844
Prevention of Terrorism Act 2005
Professional Performance Act 1995
Public Health (Control of Disease) Act 1984
Rotuli Parliamentorum, 1421, IV, 130
Sanitary Act 1866 (29 & 30 Vict. c. 90)
Sanitary Act 1868 (31 & 32 Vict. c. 115)
Sexual Offences Act 1956
Sexual Offences Act 2003

Terrorism Act 2000

Vaccination Act 1867 (30 & 31 Vict. c. 84)

Will Act 1837 (1 Vict. c. 26)

EUROPEAN LEGISLATION

Additional Protocol to the Convention for the Protection of Human Rights and the Dignity of the Human Being with regard to the Application of Biology and Medicine, on the Prohibition of Cloning Human Beings 1998

Additional Protocol to the Convention for the Protection of Human Rights and Biomedicine concerning Transplantation of Organs and Tissues of Human Origin 2002

Additional Protocol to the Convention for the Protection of Human Rights and Biomedicine concerning Genetic Testing for Health Purposes 2008

Convention for the Protection of Human Rights and Dignity of the Human Being with regard to the Application of Biology and Medicine: Convention on Human Rights and Biomedicine 1997

Directive 2005/36/EC on the Recognition of Professional Qualifications

The European Convention on Human Rights 1950

LEGISLATION (COMMONWEALTH AND OTHER JURISDICTIONS)

Constitution of the United States of America 1787

Public Law 92-603 (Social Security Act Amendment) 1973 (USA)

Rights of the Terminally Ill Act 1995 (Australia)

Termination of Life on Request and Assisted Suicide (Review Procedures) Act 2002 (Netherlands)

JOURNAL ARTICLES

Annas GJ. The art of medicine: doctors and lawyers and wolves. *Lancet.* 2008; **371**: 1832–3.

Aronson J. When I use a word . . . quacks. *BMJ*. 1997; **315** (19 July).

Bevan A. A message to the medical profession from the Minister of Health. *BMJ*. 1948; **2**: 1.

Black C. Advancing 21st-century medical professionalism. *JAMA*. 2009; **301**(20): 2156–8.

Boyd KM. Was society's response adequate in the cases of Mrs Pretty and Ms B.? *J Med Ethics*. 2002; **28**: 211–12.

Braithwaite J. New professionalism in the 21st century. *Lancet*. 2006; **367**: 645–6.

Brazier M. Patient autonomy and consent to treatment: the role of the law? *Leg Stud*. 1987; **169**: 169–93.

Bridgeman J. Young people and sexual health: whose rights? Whose responsibilities?' *Med Law Rev*. 2006; **14**(3): 418–24.

Bruce D. Regulation of doctors. *BMJ*. 2007; **334**: 436.

Catto G. The profession in the 21st century. *West Indian Med J*. 2007; **56**(3).

Catto G. Will we be getting good doctors and safer patients? *BMJ*. 2007; **334**: 450–1.

Chantler C. The role and education of doctors in the delivery of health care. *Lancet*. 1999: **353**: 1178–81.

Clark G. The history of the medical profession: aims and methods. *Med Hist*. 1966; **10**: 213–20.

Crawford MJ, Hopkins W, Thomas P *et al*. Most psychiatrists oppose plans for new mental health act. *BMJ*. 2001; **322**: 866.

Davies A. Don't trust me, I'm a doctor. *Oxf J Leg Stud*. 2000; **20**: 437–56.

Doyle L. Medical ethics and law as a core subject in medical education. *BMJ*. 1998; **316**: 1623–4.

Dyer C. Doctors lose power to regulate their profession. *BMJ*. 2007; **334**: 389.

Dyer C. GMC to introduce 'plea bargaining' for less serious misconduct cases. *BMJ*. 2007; **334**: 763.

Dyer C. Plans for revalidation are 'too complicated and aspirational'. *BMJ*. 2010; **341**: 854.

Editorial. The proposed amendment of the penal clauses of the Medical Acts. *BMJ*. 1894; **1**: 920–2.

Editorial. The nemesis of quackery. *BMJ*. 1900; **1**: 921.

Editorial. Retrospect and prospect. *BMJ*. 1948; **2**: 30–1.

Eisenberg JM. What does evidence mean? Can the law and medicine be reconciled? *J Health Polit, Policy Law*. 2001; **26**(2): 369–81.

Fallberg L. Do doctors know about their legal responsibilities? *Eur J Health Law*. 2006; **13**: 91–3.

Field S. Revalidation still moving forward, says RCGP Chair. *RCGP News*. July 2010: 1.

Godlee F. Concerns about revalidation. *BMJ*. 2006; **333**: 966–7.

Hájek O. Lord Denning and medical law. *Common Law Rev*. 2004; **5**(6).

Ham C, Alberti KGMM. The medical profession, the public, and the government. *BMJ*. 2002; **324**: 838–42.

Hughes JT. The licensing of medical practitioners in Tudor England: legislation enacted by Henry VIII. *Vesalius*. 2006; **12**(1): 4–11.

Irving D. A short history of the General Medical Council. *Med Educ*. 2006; **40**: 202–11.

Johnson J. Independence is key to better regulation. *BMJ*. 2006; **333**: 966–7.

Johnson J. Will we be getting good doctors and safer patients? *BMJ*. 2007; **334**: 450–1.

Jones M. Informed consent and other fairy tales. *Med Law Rev*. 1999; **7**: 103–34.

Kuropatnicki A. English medicine in the Tudor times. *Archiwum historii I filozofil medycyny*. 2003; **66**(2): 109–17.

Mason K, Brodie D. Bolam, Bolam – wherefore art thou Bolam? *Edin L Rev*. 2005; **9**: 298–306.

Matthews LG. London's immigrant apothecaries, 1600–1800. *Med Hist*. 1974; **18**: 262–74.

Mehlman MJ. Quackery. *Am J Law Med*. 2005; **31**: 349–63.

Morris A. Easing the passing: end of life decisions and the Medical Treatment (Prevention of Euthanasia) Bill. *Med Law Rev*. 2000; **8**: 300–15.

Porter D. Medicine and industrial society: reform, improvement, and professionalization. *Victorian Stud.* 1993; **37**(1): 129–39.

Pringle M. Regulation and revalidation of doctors. *BMJ.* 2006; **333**: 161–2.

Pringle M. Revalidation: clearer and closer. *Br J Gen Pract.* 2010; **Jul**: 475–6.

Samanta A, Samanta J. Regulation of the medical profession: fantasy, reality and legality. *JRSM.* 2004; **97**: 211–17.

Samanta A, Samanta J. Safer patients and good doctors: medical regulation in the 21st century. *Clin Risk.* 2007; **13**: 138–42.

Szmukler G. A new mental health (and public protection) act. *BMJ.* 2001; **322**: 2–3.

Simpson M, Buckman R, Stewart M *et al.* Doctor-patient communication: the Toronto consensus statement', *BMJ*, 1991; **303**: 1385–7.

Sullivan WM. Medicine under threat: professionalism and professional identity. *CMAJ.* 2000; **162**(5): 673–5.

Teff H. Consent in medical procedures: paternalism, self-determination or therapeutic alliance? *Law Q Rev.* 1985: **101**: 432.

The Law Society. Social Security Law – some legal principles in *Gillick*: A Guide – Part 1. *Law Society Gazette.* 1987; **29 Apr** (84): 1245.

Wear A. Historical keywords – quack. *Lancet.* 2005; **366**: 1157.

Whitby L. The changing face of medicine. *BMJ.* 1948; **2**: 2–6.

Woolf H. Are the courts excessively deferential to the medical profession? *Med Law Rev.* 2001; **9**(1): 1–16.

REPORTS AND DOCUMENTS

Association of Police Surgeons and the BMA. *Revised Interim Guidelines on Confidentiality for Police Surgeons in England, Wales and Northern Ireland.* London: BMA; 1998.

Bristol Royal Infirmary Inquiry. *Learning from Bristol: the report of the public inquiry into children's heart surgery of the Bristol Royal Infirmary 1984–1995.* London: HMSO; 2001.

Department of Health. *Confidentiality: NHS Code of Practice*, London: DH Publication; 2003. Available at: www.connectingforhealth.nhs.uk/systemsandservices/infogov/codes/confcode.pdf (accessed: 16 June 2010).

Department of Health. *Equality and Excellence: liberating the NHS*. London: The Stationery Office; 2010. Available at: www.dh.gov.uk/prod_consum_dh/groups/dh_digitalassets/@dh/@en/@ps/documents/digitalasset/dh_117794.pdf (accessed: 26 November 2010).

Department of Health. *Trust, Assurance and Safety – the regulation of the health professionals in the 21st century*. London: The Stationery Office; 2007. Available at: www.dh.gov.uk/prod_consum_dh/groups/dh_digitalassets/@dh/@en/documents/digitalasset/dh_065947.pdf (accessed: 30 June 2010).

Donaldson L. *Good Doctors, Safer Patients*. London: Department of Health; 2006. Available at: www.dh.gov.uk/prod_consum_dh/groups/dh_digitalassets/@dh/@en/documents/digitalasset/dh_4137276.pdf (accessed: 10 July 2010).

Foster A. *The Regulation of the Non-medical Healthcare Professions*. London: Department of Health; 2006. Available at: www.dh.gov.uk/prod_consum_dh/groups/dh_digitalassets/@dh/@en/documents/digitalasset/dh_4137295.pdf (accessed: 10 July 2010).

General Medical Council. *Confidentiality*. London: GMC; 2009.

General Medical Council. *Conflicts of Interest*. London: GMC; 2008.

General Medical Council. *Consent: patients and doctors making decisions together*. London: GMC; 2008.

General Medical Council. *Good Medical Practice*. London: GMC; 2006.

General Medical Council. *Human Fertilisation and Embryology Authority Code of Practice*. 8th ed. London: GMC; 2004.

General Medical Council. *Maintaining Boundaries*. London: GMC; 2006.

General Medical Council. *Research: the role and responsibilities of doctors*. London: GMC; 2002.

General Medical Council. *Response to Our Revalidation Consultation*. London: GMC; 2010.

General Medical Council. *Revalidation: a statement of intent.* London: GMC; 2010.

General Medical Council. *Tomorrow's Doctors.* London: GMC; 1993.

General Medical Council. *Withholding and Withdrawing Life-Prolonging Treatments: good practice in decision-making.* London: GMC; 2002.

Hansard. United Kingdom Parliament, London, 19 November 1813, Vol. 27, cols. 164–5. Available at: http://hansard.millbanksystems.com/commons/1813/nov/19/apothecaries-petition (accessed: 19 April 2010).

Hansard. United Kingdom Parliament, London, 17 June 1833, Vol. 18, cols. 912–13. Available at: http://hansard.millbanksystems.com/commons/1833/jun/17/apothecaries (accessed: 19 April 2010).

Hansard. United Kingdom Parliament, London, 11 February 1834, Vol. 21, cols. 233–6. Available at: http://hansard.millbanksystems.com/commons/1834/feb/11/the-medical-profession (accessed: 19 April 2010).

Hansard. United Kingdom Parliament, London, 11 February 1845, Vol. 77, cols. 298–304. Available at: http://hansard.millbanksystems.com/commons/1845/feb/11/medical-officers-of-poor-law-unions (accessed: 19 April 2010).

Hansard. United Kingdom Parliament, London, 25 February 1845, Vol. 77, cols. 1211–21. Available at: http://hansard.millbanksystems.com/commons/1845/feb/25/medical-profession (accessed: 19 April 2010).

Hansard. United Kingdom Parliament, London, 7 May 1845, Vol. 80, cols. 249–77. Available at: http://hansard.millbanksystems.com/commons/1845/may/07/physic-and-surgery-bill (accessed: 19 April 2010).

Hansard. United Kingdom Parliament, London, 2 July 1851, Vol. 118, cols. 111–18. Available at: http://hansard.millbanksystems.com/commons/1851/jul/02/pharmacy-bill (accessed: 19 April 2010).

Hansard. United Kingdom Parliament, London, 19 January 1996, cols. 1064–9. Available at: www.publications.parliament.uk/pa/cm199596/cmhansrd/vo950119/debtext/60119-24.htm (accessed: 10 June 2010).

Hansard. United Kingdom Parliament, London, 3 December 2002, HL Deb, Vol. 641, cols. 1098–112. Available at: http://hansard.millbanksystems.com/lords/2002/dec/03/medical-act-1983-amendment-order-2002 (accessed: 23 October 2010).

Hansard. United Kingdom Parliament, London, Medical Profession (Responsible Officers) Regulations 2010, Motion to Approve. 23 November 2010, HL Deb, cols. 1072–86. Available at: www.publications.parliament.uk/pa/ld201011/ldhansrd/text/101123-0002.htm#10112348000093 (accessed: 26 November 2010).

JM Consulting. *The Regulation of Nurses, Midwives and Health Visitors. Report on a Review on the Nurses, Midwives and Health Visitors Act 1997.* Bristol: JM Consulting Ltd; 1998.

Milburn A. House of Commons debate, 18 July 2001, Hansard, Vol. 372, cols. 289–304, Available at: http://hansard.millbanksystems.com/commons/2001/jul/18/bristol-royal-informary-inquiry (accessed: 25 September 2010).

National Clinical Assessment Agency. *Professionalism – dilemmas and lapses.* NHS National Patient Safety Agency; 2009.

NHS Litigation Authority. *NHSLA Risk Alert: informed consent.* London: NHS Litigation Authority; 2004.

The Royal Liverpool Children's Inquiry Report. London: Stationery Office; 2001. Available at: www.rlcinquiry.org.uk (accessed: 22 June 2010).

The Shipman Inquiry. London: Stationery Office; 2002. Available at: www.the-shipman-inquiry.org.uk/reports.asp (accessed: 22 June 2010).

The World Medical Association Declaration of Madrid on Professional Autonomy and Self-Regulation. [1987] 2005. Available at: www.wma.net/en/30publications/10policies/a21/index.html (accessed: 14 October 2009.)

Transactions of the Associated Apothecaries and Surgeon-Apothecaries of England and Wales. 1823. Vol. 1: xix. Available at: http://books.google.com/books?id=NgQFAAAAQAAJ&printsec=frontcover&dq=%22Transactions+of+the+Associated+Apothecaries+and+Surgeon-Apothecaries%22&num=20&ei=8cTdR6b-C4Xas-QPm3aGHDw#v=onepage&q&f=false (accessed: 25 August 2010).

Trust, Assurance, Safety – The Regulation of Health Professionals in the 21st Century. London: Stationery Office; 2007. Available at: www.dh.gov.uk/prod_consum_dh/groups/dh_digitalassets/@dh/@en/documents/digitalasset/dh_065947.pdf (accessed: 23 June 2010).

Woolf H. *Access to Justice*. London: HMSO; 1996. Available at: www.dca.gov.uk/civil/final/contents.htm (accessed: 10 July 2010).

INTERNET ARTICLES

Basketter S. Angry junior doctors take protest to the streets. *Socialist Worker* [online], 24 March 2007. Available at: www.socialistworker.co.uk/art.php?id=10982 (accessed: 11 July 2010).

Birth of NHS in Scotland: an expectant public. NHS Scotland, Scottish Government, Edinburgh. Available at: www.60yearsofnhsscotland.co.uk/history/birth-of-nhs-scotland/an-expectant-public.html (accessed: 22 June 2010).

Blackstone's Statutes on Medical Law 6th Edition: links to additional legislation. Oxford: Oxford University Press [online]. Available at: www.oup.com/uk/orc/bin/statutes/books/10medical/additional/ (accessed: 10 October 2010).

College of Physicians of London Database. British History Online. Available at: www.british-history.ac.uk/report.aspx?compid=18021 (accessed: 14 August 2010).

Compensation Culture: who's to blame? BBC News, 15 November 2000. Available at: http://news.bbc.co.uk/1/hi/uk/1024540.stm (accessed: 16 October 2010.)

Déclaration des droits de l'Homme et du Citoyen. The National Assembly of France, 26 August 1789, Article 1. Available at: www.hrcr.org/docs/frenchdec.html (accessed: 16 June 2010).

Diane Pretty Dies, BBC News, 12 May 2002. Available at: http://news.bbc.co.uk/1/hi/health/1983457.stm (accessed: 8 July 2010).

General Medical Council. *Creating a Single Regulator for Medical Education*. Available at: www.gmc-uk.org/education/postgraduate/merger.asp (accessed: 23 October 2010).

General Medical Council. *Licensing* [online]. Available at: www.gmc-uk.org/doctors/licensing.asp (accessed: 26 October 2010).

General Medical Council. Medical Act 1983 (consolidated version with amendments). Available at: www.gmc-uk.org/about/legislation/medical_act.asp (accessed: 23 October 2010).

General Medical Council. *Revalidation* [online]. Available at: www.gmc-uk.org/doctors/7330.asp (accessed: 26 October 2010).

General Medical Council. *Revalidation date set for 2012*. Press release, 18 Oct 2010. Available at: www.gmc-uk.org/news/8054.asp (accessed: 23 October 2010).

General Medical Council. *The Role of the GMC*. Available at: www.gmc-uk.org/about/role.asp (accessed: 23 October 2010).

German Court Legalises Euthanasia with Patient Consent. BBC News, 25 June 2010. Available at: http://news.bbc.co.uk/1/hi/world/europe/10414647.stm (accessed: 8 July 2010).

Iacobucci G. Responsible officers roll out gets green light. *Pulse*, 26 November 2010. Available at: www.pulsetoday.co.uk/story.asp?storycode=4127885&cid=Latest_headlines_2_261110&sp_rid=NjU3NzMzMDg0MgS2&sp_mid=36027162 (accessed: 26 November 2010).

International Association of Medical Regulatory Authorities. Available at: www.iamra.com (accessed: 23 October 2010).

Keegan L. Giving doctors the right treatment. *The Lawyer*, 21 August 2000. Available at: www.thelawyer.com/giving-doctors-the-right-treatment/104727.article (accessed: 23 October 2010).

Lambeth Palace Library. *Lambeth Palace Library Research Guide: medical licences issued by the Archbishop of Canterbury 1535–1775*. Available at: www.lambethpalacelibrary.org/files/Medical_Licences.pdf (accessed: 21 August 2010).

Martin D. Doctors' fury at government plans to release private patient data for research, Mail Online, 22 December 2008. Available at: www.dailymail.co.uk/health/article-1100385/Doctors-fury-government-plans-release-private-patient-data-research.html (accessed: 11 July 2010).

Patient Loses Right-to-Food Case, BBC News, 28 July 2005. Available at: http://news.bbc.co.uk/1/hi/health/4721061.stm (accessed: 10 July 2010).

Q&A: Terrorism Laws, BBC News, 3 July 2006. Available at: http://news.bbc.co.uk/1/hi/uk_politics/4715478.stm (accessed: 16 October 2010).

Rhodes-Kemp R. Why consent matters. *Law Society Gazette*, 6 April 2006 [online]. Available at: www.lawgazette.co.uk/opinion/comment/why-consent-matters (accessed: 4 August 2010).

Riddell M. Demonising doctors. *Guardian* [online], 4 February 2001. Available at: www.guardian.co.uk/society/2001/feb/04/health.comment (accessed: 16 October 2010).

Royal College of Physicians. College History. Available at: www.rcplondon.ac.uk/history-heritage/College-history-new/Pages/Overview.aspx (accessed: 28 June 2010).

Thompson M. *Reviews in History, No. 29: The Third Revolution. Professional elites in the modern world*. London: The Institute of Historical Research; 1997. Available at: www.history.ac.uk/reviews/review/29#t9 (accessed: 6 July 2010).

NEWSPAPERS AND MAGAZINE ARTICLES

Agate J. Demolition on Harley Street. *Daily Express*, London, 2 August 1937, p. 8.

Crisp A. Letters to the Editor. *The Daily Telegraph*, London, 2 July 2010, p. 25.

Cronin AJ. Response to James Agate. *Daily Express*, London, 5 August 1937, p. 6.

Featherstone H. GP Commissioning will be good for patients and the NHS. *The Spectator*. 13 July 2010, available at: www.spectator.co.uk/coffeehouse/6140998/gp-commissioning-will-be-good-for-patients-and-the-nhs.thtml (accessed: 26 October 2010.)

Rhodes P. Letter to the Editor. *The Times*, 12 May 1987.

Szasz T. Curing the therapeutic state. *Reason Magazine*. Los Angeles: Reason Foundation; 1963.

Verkaik R. Diane Pretty loses case, while Miss B 'dies with dignity'. *The Independent*, London, 30 April 2002.

Whitney A. A dogged legal fight to find a peaceful end. *The Independent*, London, 30 April 2002.

MISCELLANEOUS PAPERS, PERSONAL CORRESPONDENCE AND LLM ASSIGNMENTS

Jaggs-Fowler RM. *An Appraisal of Bartlett and Sandland's assertion that the 1983 Mental Health Act 'masked the reality of medical freedom with the appearance of legal controls'* [LLM assignment]. De Montfort University (unpublished); 2009.

Jaggs-Fowler RM. *A Critical Evaluation of the Majority Decision in Chester v Afshar: A sea change for information disclosure standards in English Law?* [LLM assignment]. De Montfort University (unpublished); 2010.

Index